The Sociology of
Howard S. Becker

The Sociology of
Howard S. Becker

Theory with a Wide Horizon

ALAIN PESSIN

Translated by Steven Rendall

*With a Foreword by William Kornblum
and Contributions by Howard S. Becker*

The University of Chicago Press ❋ Chicago and London

The University of Chicago Press, Chicago 60637
The University of Chicago Press, Ltd., London
© 2017 by The University of Chicago
Originally published in French as *Un sociologue en liberté: Lecture de Howard S. Becker*
© 2004 Les Presses de l'Université Laval
Published 2017
Printed in the United States of America

26 25 24 23 22 21 20 19 18 17   1 2 3 4 5

ISBN-13: 978-0-226-36271-7 (cloth)
ISBN-13: 978-0-226-36285-4 (paper)
ISBN-13: 978-0-226-36299-1 (e-book)
DOI: 10.7208/chicago/9780226362991.001.0001

Library of Congress Cataloging-in-Publication Data

Names: Pessin, Alain, author. | Becker, Howard Saul, 1928– author.
Title: The sociology of Howard S. Becker : theory with a wide horizon / Alain
    Pessin ; translated by Steven Rendall with a foreword by William Kornblum and
    contributions by Howard S. Becker.
Other titles: Sociologue en liberté. English
Description: Chicago ; London : The University of Chicago Press, 2017. | Includes
    bibliographical references.
Identifiers: LCCN 2016038509 | ISBN 9780226362717 (cloth : alk. paper) | ISBN
    9780226362854 (pbk. : alk. paper) | ISBN 9780226362991 (e-book)
Subjects: LCSH: Becker, Howard Saul, 1928– | Sociology—Philosophy.
Classification: LCC HM588 .P4713 2017 | DDC 301.01—dc23 LC record available at https://
    lccn.loc.gov/2016038509

♾ This paper meets the requirements of ANSI/NISO Z39.48–1992 (Permanence of Paper).

*To Dianne
and Catherine*

Contents

Foreword

WILLIAM KORNBLUM

Alain Pessin's intellectual biography of Howard Becker is a rare jewel of transatlantic social science. The late French sociologist argues that Becker the master sociologist has much in common with Becker the jazz improviser: both roles are played with equal intelligence and professional ease. Pessin shows us that as science, Becker's sociology is neither "soft" nor "hard" but supple. Pessin would be delighted to know that the book, originally written to give European readers more background on an American sociologist they were devouring in translation, has finally crossed the ocean. From it American readers will begin to understand why Howie Becker, our plainspoken Chicagoan, has become the world's most recognized American sociologist, while he remains the field's reigning free spirit.

For Pessin, a sociologist of art, Becker's *Art Worlds* (1982, 2008) was a seminal text. In the late eighties he sought out the always-accessible Howie in Chicago, and they remained friends until Pessin's untimely death in 2008. For the twenty-fifth anniversary edition of *Art Worlds*, Howie included an extended discussion between himself and Alain Pessin about their understandings of art as social process. But Howie not only writes about art;

in his younger years he played jazz piano in Chicago taverns. French intellectuals love jazz, and one meets French sociologists who know the history of the music and its evolving styles as well as, if not better than, their American counterparts do. When Pessin and other French sociologists attended conventions of the American Sociological Association, they would be treated to Howie's playing and struck by his generosity with amateurs who jammed with him in front of great sociological publics. His artistry at the keyboard and at the typewriter, for he is a genuine sociological stylist, helped establish Becker's rep in the free-spirit domain. But his seminal work on deviance did so even more.

Outsiders (1963) may be Becker's most enduring and original contribution to social scientific thought. Translated into all the major languages, the book has engendered a worldwide literature on deviance and labeling. In France *Outsiders* has been available for over forty years, for example, and is one of the most frequently assigned texts in French social scientific education. It was one of the Chicago volumes in the post–World War II period that called European attention to the founding intellectual traditions of American empirical sociology, Chicago style. Far from the "dust bowl empiricism" that its critics derided, the Chicago-style sociology Pessin celebrates in Becker's work is the result of many influences from within and outside the field. He finds that Becker's ideas about interaction drew from the work of his mentors and intellectual influences—Blumer, Hughes, Lindesmith, and Thomas notably—and contemporaries, including Goffman, Strauss, Vaughan, and others. He also shows how freely, like Becker's mentor Everett Hughes before him, Becker turned to the insights of nonsociologists for inspiration. Pessin cites Hughes's reading of Musil, for example, and describes how Becker drew inspiration from Georges Perec and Italo Calvino.

Howie's is the treasured voice of the third generation of Chicago sociologists. But in contrast to earlier midwestern sociology (often the straitlaced product of parsons' sons), Becker, Goffman, Cavan, the Loflands, Strauss, Suttles, and the pioneering researchers on sexual interaction Gagnon and Simon opened the field to research on human behavior that was free of moral prejudices and the limitations of superficial samples. But is Becker lacking in theoretical chops, as some who demand extensive "theorization" of the issues they study claim? Bruno Latour, no stranger to theory of any appellation, argues the contrary: "There is in fact in Becker's approach a perfectly theorized manner of not having theory." Latour admires Becker's theoretical and methodological stance in *Art Worlds*, for example, for it allows Becker to observe how meanings emerge from seemingly disparate practices among participants in social situations.[1] For American sociologists, like those in the urban ethnography network, led from Yale by the inspiring Elijah Anderson, a former student of Becker's, Howie's work offers endless examples of how to make sense of fieldwork observations, which are always rich in meanings, mysteries, and political implications.

Pessin and other French sociologists were similarly drawn to Becker's supple ethnographic analysis of social phenomena, in contrast to the "heavier," more institutionally deterministic traditions of French sociology, as defined by Durkheim and later by Becker's contemporary the late Pierre Bourdieu. In his 2015 *New Yorker* profile of Howard ("Howie") Becker, Adam Gopnick observed that Becker's "books became a magnetic pole around which dissident French sociologists could gather," and the books, as well as the research stance they advocated, "provided a means to combat the man who, for a generation, had been the dominant figure in French social science, Pierre Bourdieu." Becker explained to Gopnick that

> Bourdieu's big idea was the *champs*, field, and mine was *monde*, world—what's the difference? Bourdieu's idea of field is kind of mystical. It's a metaphor from physics. I always imagined it as a zero-sum game being played in a box. The box is full of little things that zing around. And he doesn't speak about people. He just speaks about forces. There aren't any people doing anything. Mine is a view that—well, it takes a village to write a symphony and get it performed.[2]

The free spirit in Becker refuses ever to be bound by prior assumptions about what should be happening or who should be acting or reacting. This methodological stance is especially attractive to students tired of theoretical orientations that promise to yield few new insights. For Becker the trick is to look carefully and then be able to explain what has happened in the terms of those who created the action or the scene. Sociologists who go into the field with axes to grind or theories to prove usually find uninspiring confirmation of preconceived ideas. Since 2004, when Pessin's intellectual biography of Becker was published in Europe, Becker has published a number of highly successful books about working in and writing about the social sciences. Most of these have been translated into French and other European languages and are assigned to students entering sociological research programs. This is also true for many graduate social science programs in the United States, where Becker's work on sociological methods and writing in the social sciences is required reading and has helped stimulate a new generation of keenly observed and clearly written empirical studies on a wide variety of subjects.

In *"Do You Know . . . ?" The Jazz Repertoire in Action* (2009), his empirical work on repertoire and improvisation (coauthored with jazz trumpet player and sociologist Robert Faulkner), Howie delights in the give-and-take of spontaneous conversation, be it musical or verbal. Fortunately, some strands of his rich sociological conversations with French social scientists were gathered in print by Alain Pessin and a colleague, Alain Blanc, in 2004, shortly before Pessin's death. Entitled (my translation from the French) *Art of the Field: A Medley Offered to Howard S. Becker* (*L'art du terrain: Mélanges offerts à Howard S. Becker*), the collection includes, to cite only one example, a charming essay by Pessin in which he seeks to explain to his American friend Howie Becker the intricacy and beauty of the social world of French long-distance cycling and the heroes who reigned over it before the "social construction of Lance Armstrong." A few years earlier, in 1999, on the occasion of an honorary doctorate awarded to

Howie by Pierre Mendès-France University, in Grenoble, Pessin and colleagues produced a volume in French (*Paroles et musique*) in which Howie outlines many of the ideas about jazz as art that he later expanded in his work with Rob Faulkner. The text is accompanied by a recorded jazz session featuring Howie on piano and the brilliant French bassist Benoît Cancoin. It is another example of how keenly Howie is appreciated in France and how his own work has been influenced by French colleagues' attention to his oeuvre.

In recent years Howie and his wife, Dianne, a skilled photojournalist, divide their time between San Francisco and Paris. Although their popularity among French social scientists can certainly be explained by Howie's standing as a renowned sociologist, the couple's obvious delight in French culture is also always in evidence. As one who has had the privilege of spending time with them in Paris, I can say that French and other European scholars also choose to spend hours with Howie and Dianne in Parisian bistros and cafés or in their homes because they can all converse in French. Friends and professional peers, they share stories from the field, but they understand themselves to be speaking with someone whose intellectual pedigree extends through three generations of American sociology (with a Chicago twist). Few living sociologists have this distinction. Few are the subject of an intellectual biography. None deserve the honor more than Howard S. Becker, Chicago's "Howie."

Prologue

For a jazz concert, you need more than a few musicians and a group of people who have come to listen to them. There also have to be other musicians who have constructed and finally established the kind of musical practice that is called "jazz"; musical choices must have been made that designate the act of playing this kind of music as worthy of collective interest, instrumental ensembles must have been recognized as suitable for this kind of music, people and societies have to have perfected and produced the instruments and made them commercially available; jazz music has to have become shareable, and for that, first of all, even before we can speak of the existence of a musical sensibility for this genre during a given period in given social groups, sheet music and recordings have to have been made and distributed, and the producers of radio programs have to have chosen to broadcast this artistic expression.

In addition, a concert requires people to seek venues where musicians and audiences can meet, to sell tickets at the entrance, and to set up the lighting and sound systems; the concert has be advertised and, without going through the whole list of all the actors involved, there has to be a parking attendant. The latter, no matter how modest—and profane, some would say—his participation might be, is just as essential as the others: as essential as the artists and the music lovers who are eager to hear them, because if there is no parking attendant, there is no parking, no one can get to the site of the event, and there is no concert and no music.

This example, which is often found in Howard S. Becker's sociology, clearly shows that even in the domain of art—which is supposed to be the domain of select passions that people would like to think are independent of material contingencies—the production of events, of works of art, and the actualization of these valued select passions are the result of a collective effort, an organized activity that generally involves a large number of actors, including actors whose role is small but without whom nothing is possible, neither a jazz concert nor any other artistic expression, nor for that matter any manifestation of social life in general.

What we have to call jazz, or music—and this holds for any collective event—is the result at a given time of all these coordinated activities and of all the choices that are made in connection with them. If on a given day jazz brings us together, that is because a complex series of activities has made it a kind of music that we have learned to accept and to like and because decisions and investments on the part of men and women have made it possible for jazz to continue to exist. And like everything else, it will exist only as long as somebody is engaged in it.

A sociology of jazz is therefore first of all a sociology of the social activity through which jazz is actualized as a shareable musical object. It has to account for all the interactions through which this shareable character of an object was constructed.

Even if it plays an important role in Becker's work, the example of jazz is not merely anecdotal here. I could have taken any other example—an educational relationship, the making of a political decision, a family situation—any of these would have led to this necessity of considering the coordinated activity of the whole set of actors concerned, and it is only at the end of their collaboration (whatever form is given to it, whether voluntarily cooperative or conflictual) that the facts with which sociologists are usually thought to be concerned are conventionally defined: works of art between their production and their reception, the procedures and results of the transmission of knowledge, the fact of power and all the problems connected with it, marriage, divorce, family recompositions, and so on.

This strong inflection Becker gives to sociology is also found at work in all the themes he took up successively, among which art and deviancy occupy an essential position. Before going into detail concerning the various phenomena that aroused Becker's sociological curiosity, let us adhere for the moment to this orientation: "We can define sociology as the study of the way people do things together."[1]

Becker does sociology. He also does other things, especially music: he has been a professional jazz pianist since he was young, and even if his musical career has had less intense moments in the meantime, in 2003 he recorded a CD.[2] He does photography, cooks, and participates in theater, to name only a few of his interests. But in the end, we consider him a sociologist. In accord with his own conception of social activity, a man who has become one of the best-known sociologists in the world, a permanent participant in so many debates that roil contemporary sociology, cannot have done all that by himself.

The question that will guide us is therefore this: with whom could Becker do sociology, in Chicago and other places, in the second half of the twentieth century, and with whom is he still doing it today? By choosing this point of view, this kind of "reading" of Becker's work, I seek precisely to oppose the idea of an oeuvre that is valuable only because of its ultimate results—its theoretical results, that is, the ones that can be generalized and isolated from the collective procedure through which they were obtained. I seek to avoid the illusion of a scientific work that produces the illusion that it is autonomous.

On the contrary, I want to pay homage to Becker's work by understanding the word in the American sense of effort, activity. Becker's sociology is fertile chiefly because it constantly seeks to question the world and also to doubt sociological reflexes, ready-made ways of approaching problems that encumber and hobble the way sociologists question the world. Becker's work, like any work, is carried out in given circumstances, in particular situations, confronted by specific people coming from diverse social milieus.

In this gallery of Becker's accomplices, we find first of all musicians. In the 1950s and 1960s, in Chicago and a few other cities, he was a "Saturday night musician." For dances, private parties, bar mitzvahs, and in nightclubs, taverns, and strip joints, he spent whole nights behind the piano and even learned to keep on playing as he took a little nap. The musical ambitions of these groups, often cobbled together at the last moment with musicians who did not know each other, were generally quite limited: doing what they had to do to be hired again, in other combinations, week after week. Playing jazz—these musicians' only declared ambition—for audiences and employers who didn't think much of this kind of music was a kind of compromise.[3] This collective establishment of an arrangement based on shareable music was to provide first-rate autobiographical material for the writing of *Art Worlds*.

Becker's students should also be mentioned, because discussions in his classes often clarified his ideas and shaped his books.

Finally, there are his teachers and his colleagues. Everett C. Hughes and Herbert Blumer played the role of teachers, but the whole great Chicago tradition passed through them and outlined Becker's intellectual family tree:

> Studying at the University of Chicago was an enormous advantage for me, and certainly put its stamp on my way of thinking about sociology. We could trace a kind of genealogical lineage: I studied a great deal with Everett Hughes, who taught me what I know about social organization; and Hughes had studied with Robert Park, who, in turn, had been Georg Simmel's student. There you have my "family history." The other branch runs through Herbert Blumer, with whom I studied social psychology; if we go back up the genealogical tree on that side, we find George Herbert Mead, John Dewey, and William James. With Lloyd Warner, we go back to Radcliffe-Brown

and Durkheim. But what really excited me in social anthropology was not so much the theory as the romantic side of the fieldwork. Studying and observing the life of individuals or groups, in detail and over long periods. In that sense, my tastes haven't changed since that time. All my studies, including *Art Worlds*, are closely connected with direct, personal experience.[4]

Let us take Becker at his word: he is the one who tells us that we can understand things in the social world only by looking at how they are done together. We will see how his own work "does things together." That will be the most faithful way of describing it.

1

People Who Get High and the Others

Chicago, Illinois

If Becker is right in saying that sociological activity is a kind of work like any other and owes its results at least as much to the complexity of its collective organization as to the exceptional astuteness of certain individuals, then an innovative sociological result can occur only in a situation that favors it and involves both chains of cooperation and accidental innovations. *Outsiders*, the book that first brought Becker international recognition, fully confirms this point of view.

The research environment at Chicago was propitious for such a scientific coincidence. There was a very old tradition of research on delinquency that had given rise to many studies that were constantly developing and revising their area of investigation. Becker was not one of these sociologists of delinquency, and never became one. He worked, along with others, on problems in the sociology of occupations. Just before *Outsiders* appeared, he had published, in collaboration with Blanche Geer, Everett Hughes, and Anselm Strauss, *Boys in White: Student Culture in Medical School*, which focused on students' collective resistance to the academic and intellectual demands and requirements the professors imposed on them. But it was by importing this point of view of the sociology of occupations into what the sociology of delinquency had belatedly become that he could carry out a major reorientation of research in this domain through his use of the term "deviancy," the deployment of the notion of "career," and what was to called, despite his opposition, "labeling theory." The originality of this reorientation is certain, but it is also relative, because Becker made use of an interpretive scheme that was easily identifiable as belonging to the Chicago School's tradition.[1]

The theme of delinquency as a consequence of "social disorganization" had been discussed since the early 1920s by many researchers and fieldworkers, often in the twofold sense of sociology and social activism. Social disorganization, which resulted not only in delinquency but also in divorce and abandonment of families, suicide, alcoholism, and other problems, was for them a particularly catastrophic effect, particularly for disadvantaged youths, of the constant and rapid transformations of the modern metropolis. Thomas and Znaniecki's pioneering work on Polish immigrants[2] blazed a trail followed by Park, by Burgess, and, after them, by many others, including Thrasher, who analyzed gangs, and Shaw and McKay. The premise long shared by these studies was that "delinquency among the young is a consequence of the loss of the influence of the social control exercised by traditional institutions such as churches, the family, and local communities, under the new conditions encountered in cities by emigrants of rural origin."[3]

Jean-Michel Chapoulie maintains that one of the factors enabling us to understand the transition, in the 1950s, from the notion of social disorganization to the notion of deviancy is the professionalization of Chicago sociology, which involved greater detachment with respect to social action.[4] After Sutherland began analyzing the notion of crime outside the milieu of young people from poor immigrant backgrounds, focusing instead on white-collar crime, Becker could seek an illustration of what was henceforth called "deviance" in situations that were less sociologically typified, less marked by the weight of macrosociology, and in more fluid practices. In his work, deviance was to be seen as the result of choices, of situations characterized by less predictable interactions that were much less easily associated with the oppressive constraints of a destiny that was not chosen. The preconditions for deviance were no longer a generalized anomie or a serious social disorganization. Deviance is virtually everywhere and is an everyday, normal social fact. It is even reasonable to ask, Becker notes, what keeps people from being more deviant than they are:

> There is no reason to assume that only those who finally commit a deviant act actually have the impulse to do so. It is much more likely that most people experience deviant impulses frequently. At least in fantasy, people are much more deviant than they appear. Instead of asking why deviants want to do things that are disapproved of, we might better ask why conventional people do not follow through on the deviant impulses they have.[5]

This reorientation of the sociologist's approach makes it possible to move from investigations that are necessarily more general, sometimes have a strong collective moral goal, and in any case are always solidly anchored in the current social drama of a great, anomic city to a more flexible kind of investigation and more minute analyses of particular cases connected with the overall context by ramifications more delicate but just as propitious, even though in a different way, for the invention of approaches valuable for sociology in general. Becker drew such approaches from direct observation and interviews with marijuana smokers and dance musicians. It is very clear that for these two groups, which obviously intersect in part, no characterization as "victims" of the general anomie can be taken seriously. How is the experience of "getting high," that is, drawing as much pleasure as possible from smoking marijuana, constructed? How do people persist, despite the pressures and obstacles, in playing "real music," that is, jazz? These apparently anecdotal questions are nonetheless capable of authorizing the formulation of general hypotheses regarding deviancy, if they are approached with the proven persistence and ingenuity of the Chicago School's questioning.

Deviance in Deviance

The fertility of a sociological enterprise has in large part to do with the sociologist's ability to transform or overturn the questions that are usually asked about the reality concerned. Becker frequently returns to his teacher Herbert Blumer's way of seeing each stage in the construction of sociological knowledge in terms of representations. "Blumer thought, and so do I, that the basic operation in studying society—we start with images and end with them—is the production and refinement of an image of the thing we are studying."[6]

In the case of deviancy, the representations that were available to a young researcher in the early 1950s converged on the intrinsically deviant character of the act and its actor. Scientific theories and common sense asked the same question: "Why do some people transgress the norm?" And they gave the same reply: it is because some people are substantially deviant that they decide to commit acts that are themselves substantially deviant.[7] Such a conception implies that the norm is not the object of a decision, that it is received as such from some authority outside the social, given once and for all and beyond question. Here the norm is taken for granted, and only perverse forces might try to transgress it.

But obviously the norm cannot be taken for granted. Different groups do not describe the same actions as deviant, and the same policeman does not always treat the same acts with the same severity, depending, for instance, on whether the person shoplifting candy is black or white. A better question is "Who defines the norm, and under what conditions do those who define it undertake to ensure that it is respected?"

Such a relativization of the norm allows us to assess the representations given us at the start. Considering the norm as an objective given, sociologists merely accepted existing values and continued the action of those who defined the norm in a given place and at a given moment. Sociology has not the slightest chance of gaining a clear view of collective actions if it does not methodically tear itself away from the established powers by asking questions different from the conventional ones asked by institutions.

The norm is now considered a collective commitment. We can grasp it more correctly by taking into account not only the act itself but also the way it is seen, as well as the reciprocity of the ways the various actors involved in the act see it. If a social group considers a deviant an outsider, the latter can also reject the norm that is used against him and consider the group in question as foreign to his own universe.[8]

The norm is part of a dynamic schema. The new point of view set up here consists in making the very existence of deviance inseparable from the many procedures through which people observe, assess, designate, and label it. If the norm is relative, if it corresponds only to a choice made by certain groups, then deviance is also absolutely relative, and we can evaluate it only by the standard of the norm producers' way of seeing things, by the standard of those whom Becker calls the "entrepreneurs of morality": a behavior can be considered deviant only because someone has set up a barrier at that point and accuses someone else of crossing it. Whence the initial viewpoint of *Outsiders*:

> I . . . view deviance as the product of a transaction that takes place between some social group and one who is viewed by that group as a rule-breaker. I will be less concerned with the personal and social characteristics of deviants than with the process by which they come to be thought of as outsiders and their reactions to that judgment.[9]

Deviance as a Process of Symbolic Creation

Now we are dealing with a new representation of the phenomenon of deviance. An act—taking drugs, engaging in an illicit sexuality, stealing from a charitable organization, killing one's professor, or whatever it might be—is no longer seen as being by itself the organizer of the social behaviors of those who perform it and those who oppose it but is, rather, understood as organized by a complex set of social activities whose fragile result it is. As an object that transmits meaning, it is constructed in a set of interactions. It results from the latter as an elaboration that has to be carried out over and over under increasingly complex and changing collective conditions. The sociological object "deviance" is not an inventory of behaviors or a statistic reporting their frequency: it is a symbolic object constructed through a collective process that is symbolic in the sense that it is something that unites us, at a given time, in a common meaning.

Thus, deviance, like everything else, is something we do together. And it can be understood only by examining the roles played in the production of this meaning by all the parties involved. This is a permanent viewpoint in Becker's work; he demands that all the interactions in a social landscape (which may vary in size) be taken into account. In his later work on artistic practices, this requirement leads to a clarification of the notion of a "world."

Consider the way all the actors involved participate, together, in the definition of deviance, the act of definition having symbolic efficacy and thus very practical consequences. Saying that deviance unites all these actors is an example sufficient to settle a minuscule problem: that of the term "cooperation," which is often used by Becker but is also used in speaking about him to make the objection that ties of this kind may also be manifested, and commonly, by opposition and sometimes by conflict. It is fair to say that all the actors cooperate in the symbolic production of deviance. But in this precise case, it is only too easy to see that they by no means do so in the mode of professional or friendly fraternization. Here they oppose one another, seek each other out or avoid one another, fight with one another. But that is, of course, a modality of cooperation just like fraternization or any other variation on "doing things together."

The debate regarding the term "labeling theory" is another small point that can be settled here. The success of *Outsiders* was accompanied by a misunderstanding. People wanted to see the book as the most complete expression of a "labeling theory," as if we could say—and this is what this compact expression might suggest—that the deviant character of an action derives solely from the fact that it is considered at a certain moment to be deviant. Understanding Becker's work as based on a "labeling theory" is obviously restrictive and erroneous. Independent of the fact that it overhastily describes as a *theory* a sociological work that, as I shall discuss later on, is deeply wary of theorizing, it reduces the complex reality of deviance to a single act. In the case of Becker, this reduction was the most inappropriate one possible because if his work contains the basis for a theory, it consists precisely in establishing that it is never possible to reduce a situation to a single act, that a "social fact," whatever it might be, always proceeds from multiple interactions—in other words, from diverse intentions that intersect and combine.

Becker constantly insists on the limited nature of his statements. It would be absurd to think that deviance is created by the simple act of labeling it. It is not solely because they are labeled as such that marijuana smokers go on smoking, although it does constitute an important element in the development of this practice. Moreover, Becker did not seek to account for all aspects of deviance. He limited himself to proposing a point of view, which was original at that time,[10] that made by definition no claim to exhaust the phenomenon but that did shed light on an essential aspect of it: the cooperation of multiple actors in symbolic acts that play an active role in the development of deviant practices. And it is very true that his point of departure consisted in drawing attention to the fact that to understand deviance, the objection formulated against it has to be included.

That being the case, although Becker called for balance in future studies of deviance, which he hoped would discuss with the same interest those who transgressed norms and those who issued and applied them, the reproach he addressed to "most of the research and scientific speculations on deviancy," that is, focusing almost exclusively on the transgressors, could to a certain extent be turned against him. For if he is determined to summon before the bar of judgment all the actors involved in the production of deviance, most of his book is devoted to the transgressors,

with only a rather short chapter on the "entrepreneurs of morality." This chapter is moreover too brief to give more than a very
general idea of these entrepreneurs' action, and no doubt a rather
restrictive one, since only the problem of "moral crusades" and of
their policing-related consequences is mentioned in it, as if the
norm were only and always a moral limit. Can't it also be a set
of practical limits, discreet but tenacious requirements to toe the
line regarding conventional ways of doing things, a normalizing
pressure that does not imply a crusade but pervades everyday
life? However, as a sociologist working in the field, Becker was
probably less interested in this aspect of things than in the subtle
nuances that are constructed through a deviant career.

The Stages of the Deviant Career

The interactionist approach is probably most clearly defined by
the fact that the actor's behavior is not seen as the final outcome
of a set of variables but rather as a process through which the actor constantly defines and redefines his relation to his social environment. So we can say that the meaning of acts is *constructed*,
using the word "meaning" in the sense that has been common up
to now: meaning is what results from a collective effort to classify
things—for example, to classify what is deviant and what is not.
Thus, this procedure can hardly limit itself to tools like those of
multivariate analysis, which presupposes that

> all the factors contributing to the production of the phenomenon
> studied act simultaneously; it seeks to discover the variable, or the
> combination of variables, that will best "predict" the behavior con-
> cerned. For example, in a study on juvenile delinquency, an effort will
> be made to discover whether it is the child's IQ, the neighborhood
> where he lives, the break-up of his family, or some combination of
> these factors, that accounts for his delinquency.[11]

However, not only do all these factors not act at the same time,
but a deviant's career encompasses successive states that call for
new analyses of the situation, a reconsideration of what links the

actor and his action to partners and to the social circumstances that surround him. Thus, it turns out to be more effective to choose a sequential model and to try to understand what the stages of deviance consist in, whether they concern those who are fully deviant (transgressing the norm and perceived as deviant), those who are secretly deviant (transgressing the norm but not perceived as deviant), or those who are wrongly accused of deviancy (obeying the norm and perceived as deviant).[12]

In the notion of a career, developed by occupational sociology, Becker finds an adequate instrument:

> In the study of occupations, where this concept was first worked out, it refers to the series of movements from one position to another made by a worker in an occupational system. It also includes the idea of events and circumstances affecting the career. This notion designates the factors on which the mobility from one position to another depends, that is, both objective facts pertaining to the social structure and changes in the individual's prospects, motivations, and desires.[13]

In his definition of the idea of a career, Hughes resolutely connects the objective dimension (the series of statuses or positions successively occupied) and the subjective dimension, that is, "the changes in the perspective in accord with which the person perceives his existence as a totality and interprets the meaning of his diverse characteristics and actions, along with everything that happens to him."[14]

We see that the term "career" imported into the domain of deviance promises to become commonly used in general sociology. It is not intended to be applied solely to professional deviants: it can be applied to every passage through deviance, no matter how episodic and trivial it may be, because it refers, in a general way, to a graduated process that requires at every stage a transformation of the representation of the situation.

The first stage in a deviant career is particularly interesting, because it forces us to unravel the processes of social engagement and disengagement. Obviously, there are different ways of becoming a deviant. For various reasons—whether one lacks a clear awareness of the extent of the application of the norm and performs an act without knowing that one is violating the norm, or whether one is participating in a subculture that masks the real operation of the norm in the group he belongs to—people can perform acts that disobey the norm without intending to do so.[15] This figure of the accidental deviant is another case to be added to the three types already mentioned.

But, of course, intentional deviance attracts more interest. What does it presuppose? What steps have to be taken to achieve it? And what are the consequences of these steps for the apprentice deviant? We cannot avoid referring to a first time. Was the way for it prepared by latent desires, long-repressed unconscious needs that nonetheless one day led an individual to act and satisfy his desire, simply because that was the condition of his personal equilibrium? That is an avenue of analysis often pursued, as we know. It is remarkable that it hardly interests Becker at all. As we have seen, he rejects the notion that deviants constitute a separate category of individuals whose future deviance is foreseeable on the basis of causes that concern them alone, because of what has constituted or still constitutes their psychic or social lives. He refuses to concede that deviants are thus designated in advance, a little cohort doomed, by powerful determining factors they do not understand or control, to realize themselves, as was their destiny, in deviance. He thinks, as we know, that most people can be deviant, are tempted to be deviant, are on the point of becoming deviant—but nonetheless only a few actually become deviant.

How do they become deviant? Becker's analysis, and generally that of interactionism, puts the emphasis, like no other trend in sociology, on the notion of situation: What is happening at a given moment? How are the various temptations a person is experiencing at this moment resolved? This analysis indisputably prevails over those based on accumulated experiences. To see how someone comes to act, we have to imagine a kind of disengagement, something that gives him the opportunity and the strength to escape his conditioning, his routines, and the reproduction of the foreseeable. This ability to overthrow, by giving priority to a strong temptation, the representation that one has of his own situation in collective life is a decisive element that alone can authorize us to conceive of change, in this case a radical change in individual behavior.

The process of engagement is in no way surprising:

> We can consider the normal history of individuals in our society (and probably in any society) as a series of increasingly numerous and deep engagements with regard to conventional norms and institutions. When a "normal" individual discovers in himself a deviant temptation, he is capable of repressing it by thinking of the multiple consequences that would ensue if he yielded to it; remaining normal represents too important a stake for him to allow himself to be influenced by deviant temptations.[16]

But what does yielding to deviant temptations entail? What makes it possible? The case of a marginality with respect to norms, of an adventurous freedom of spirit maintained since childhood, can exist, but it contributes rather little to the debate. Far more interesting is the troubled situation in which the temptation to remain in conformity with the norms ends up being disqualified by action.

To account for the possibility of the latter, Becker appeals to the analyses of Gresham Sykes and David Matza, which, though they are interesting, nonetheless confine the problem to the particular level of the resolution of what social psychologists call "cognitive dissonance." Renouncing your ability to act and to see yourself as tossed about, completely powerless, from one situation to another, in order at the same time to discharge yourself of your responsibility; minimizing the consequences your act may have on others; deciding that your victims deserve what they get and that all the damage you might do to them can ultimately be seen as a good thing, given their perverted and unhealthy nature—these are a few of the mental techniques by means of which a situation of cognitive dissonance can be resolved.

But there is more; there is another level, which pertains to general sociology and at which two things are going on at the same time. The first thing is rupture, an opening to the unprecedented. I will come back to this and stress its importance, because in Becker's sociology it marks a position radically contrary to those held for more than a century by sociology in general and especially by a certain trend in French sociology that posits that individuals' behaviors can arise only from the interiorization, the assimilation or incorporation of norms, which in turn suggests that we really can desire only what has been inculcated socially in us as desirable. Instead of that, here it is understood, and this constitutes a basis for reflection, that the norm always remains external to individuals and is an object of interindividual negotiation; that free, roaming desire always exists in everyone; that therefore there is a permanent capacity for rupture, for disengagement, for the exploration of possible situations.

This presupposition of availability is not presented in Becker's work as something that participates in a theory of the social. He expresses this point of view with the greatest force when he describes it as a practical procedure, one of his "tricks of the trade." It is Hughes's trick, or at least one of his tricks. It can be summed up in these words: everything is possible.

> Everett Hughes taught me a wonderful trick. . . . He liked to quote the hero of Robert Musil's novel, *The Man without Qualities*, saying "Well, after all, it could have been otherwise." We should never assume that anything is impossible, simply could not happen. Rather, we ought to imagine the wildest possibilities and then wonder why they don't happen.[17]

Becker's constant insistence on disengagement or rupture—his affirmation that everything could have "happened differently" and that everything still can happen differently, at any time—did not proceed from a value judgment but from the point of view of practical sociology.

A second way to understand deviance as constituted by acting on temptations and desires is to realize that unless it remains purely anecdotal and has no consequences, acting inaugurates a new engagement. In other words—and Becker demonstrates this powerfully in the example of marijuana smokers, an example to which I'll soon return—the deviant's career, even in its initial phase, and at the same time that it is a process of rupture, is already a process of socialization:

> Before engaging in the activity on a more or less regular basis, the person has no notion of the pleasures to be derived from it; he learns these in the course of interaction with more experienced deviants. He learns to be aware of new kinds of experiences and to think of them as pleasurable. What may well have been a random impulse to try something new becomes a settled taste for something already known and experienced. The vocabularies in which deviant motivations are phrased reveal that their users acquire them in interactions with other deviants. The individual *learns*, in short, to participate in a subculture organized around the particular deviant activity.[18]

A crucial new stage is the one in which the individual is caught and publicly recognized as deviant. The chief consequence of this is others' awareness of the change in the status, in the identity, of the individual concerned. Becker adopts Hughes's distinction between master statuses and auxiliary statuses. The master status (which is often occupational) is the one on the basis of which others' presumptions regarding the whole set of ways of acting, and regarding the different aspects of someone's personality, are formed. Changing the master status (ceasing to be an honest cashier and becoming one who dips into the till) implies that everything that person does will be assumed to be in profound accord with the character he has just been discovered to have.

This process of the unification of statuses is full of practical consequences. It becomes increasingly difficult for the person concerned to take part in the life of nondeviant groups. Seeing himself excluded, particularly from opportunities for regular employment, he will find himself obliged to increase his deviance by using illegal means to ensure his subsistence. Here we have a particularly clear example of the efficacy of interactions that unite the deviant with those who designate him as such.

Finally, a later stage, marked by new learning processes and new reinforcements, is that of the entrance into an organized deviant group. It is the latter that

> gives them a sense of common fate, of being in the same boat. From a sense of common fate, from having to face the same problems, grows a deviant subculture: a set of perspectives and understandings about what the world is like and how to deal with it and a set of routine activities based on those perspectives. Membership in such a group solidifies a deviant identity.[19]

This process is illustrated by examples drawn from fieldwork. I will examine here only the most famous example, the one concerning the set of interactions at work in an individual's persistence in seeking the pleasure of "getting high" through the effects of marijuana.

Marijuana Smokers' Experience

The pleasure in question here is very far from being a pure product of the chemical action of a substance on the person who consumes it. Becker shows that only a complex social process allows smokers to enjoy this pleasure, a process that naturally involves all the actors concerned in the symbolic definition of this kind of deviance.[20] It is marked by stages and thus establishes a kind of career. At each stage, the smoker learns to resolve a certain number of problems connected with the use of marijuana. These problems are related to the substance itself, to partners who smoke, and various social controls that disapprove of smoking.

How does one become a regular smoker? The example of marijuana is interesting for two reasons. The first is that it is a "soft" drug that does not lead to dependency. All studies show that, unlike harder drugs like tobacco or alcohol, marijuana can be consumed in a very episodic manner and given up for long periods of time; in short, it does not subject its users to the everyday constraints associated with the phenomenon of addiction.

Becoming a regular smoker is thus connected with something other than the drug's physical influence on everyday life.

On the other hand, the effects of marijuana are not very clear. People's first impressions of it are strange, sometimes frightening, and thus we cannot maintain that it responds, of itself, to a motivation that is already present. Between trying it for the first time and being a regular user, there is a necessary learning process. Becker shows that this process can only be social and corresponds in reality to the construction of a motivation. Far from preceding the experience, the motivation is worked out in the experience. Here again Becker's sociology gives priority to actual situations as instituting and distributing meaning:

> Instead of the deviant motive leading to the deviant behavior, it is the other way around; the deviant behavior in time produces the deviant motivation. Vague impulses and desires—in this case, probably most frequently a curiosity about the kind of experience the drug will produce—are transformed into definite patterns of action through the social interpretation of a physical experience which is in itself ambiguous. Marijuana use is a function of the individual's conception of marijuana and of the uses to which it can be put, and this conception develops as the individual's experience with the drug increases.[21]

It is through interactions with other smokers that an individual is able, step-by-step, to become a regular smoker. Such meetings and confrontations with other smokers are practically inevitable in the situation we are concerned with here.

The second reason that the case of marijuana is especially interesting is that the authorities (the social controls) limit access to marijuana and disrupt sources of supply, so that you have to go to illicit sources to get the drug, which means that you have to deal with organized networks, even if only as a simple customer. Thus, it is unlikely that anyone can begin to smoke without joining a group that provides access to these sources.

The novice therefore lives in fear of being caught and of suffering the damaging effects (in his activities and in his affective life) of being designated a deviant. But this fear can be attenuated, notably by observing the apparent calm manifested by regular smokers. This becomes another reason to hang out with them.

Above all, one can continue to smoke only if one has learned how to do it, and this can be done only under the tutelage of experienced smokers. At first, one cannot know much about the drug's effects. All one knows is that other people use it regularly and say that they take pleasure in it, the pleasure of "getting high." But what is "getting high"? In what does this pleasure consist? The new user has little chance of discovering that by himself. Generally speaking, his experiences will be disconcerting so long as he has not learned the techniques, particularly those of dosage and inhalation, which once mastered will allow him to get high.

Finally, even if the beginner goes about it in the right way, he cannot feel the necessary effects. Here again a learning process is necessary to recognize the effects produced by the consumption of marijuana. At first one can get high and not realize it, because one does not know the forms that the experience of getting high is supposed to take, as attested by others. It is only when the novice becomes capable of getting high (i.e., of identifying certain symptoms as those associated with that experience) that he is inclined to smoke for pleasure:

> With increasing experience the user develops a greater appreciation of the drug's effects; he continues to learn to get high. He examines succeeding experiences closely, looking for new effects, making sure the old ones are still there. Out of this grows a stable set of categories for experiencing the drug's effects whose presence enables the user to get high with ease.[22]

That is when he has become a connoisseur.

The smoker then has to stop being dependent on an episodic and dangerous supply of the drug. He has to find stable sources that can be counted on to supply him reliably and safely. But, above all, he has to take another step in learning the relationship between his body and the substance he is using: he has to learn to like the effects of what he has become capable of feeling. He has to learn to take pleasure in what he feels, which is by no means self-evident.

Here again nothing can replace the support of experienced smokers who are capable of providing reassurance, of confirming that they have also experienced identical sensations, which may be difficult or frightening, and have overcome them, and who are capable of helping the learner dissociate the pleasant from the unpleasant and to limit the amount of smoke absorbed in order to eliminate the uncomfortable symptoms as much as possible.

The transition to regular use of marijuana is once again a thoroughly social operation. Smoking frequently, and whenever one wants to, implies having to be high in the presence of nonsmokers, in the presence of one's coworkers or one's family. That is always an ordeal, and a further learning process is required to understand that it is possible to hold up one's end of a conversation or carry out a task—that is, to continue to deceive others—while being high. Another solution consists, obviously, in frequenting only groups of smokers. In all cases, the smokers' milieu constitutes its own subculture and does so in part by perfecting rationalizations and justifications of its own deviancy.

2

Jazzmen and Company

It was with Everett Hughes, who recognized a pertinent sociological approach in Becker's interest in artistic practices, and in the company of numerous musicians (who were, like him, Saturday night jazzmen obliged to compromise with employers and an audience that had little desire to listen to jazz) that our sociologist-pianist elaborated his conception of "art worlds," which is now a permanent element and a necessary reference in debates about the sociology of art all over the world.

It is probably no exaggeration to say that all this work was ultimately done only to answer a single question, a simple and practical question but one that implies a methodically constructed response, an overall hypothesis concerning all artistic practices. This question is the following: how do Saturday night musicians—who gather for a musical evening in ways that are neither very regular nor repetitive, who thus usually do not know each other half an hour before playing the first set, and who thus have not been able to rehearse at all—manage to play together and stop together?

Answering this question implies a general reflection on what it is to "do art," on the organization of the artistic occupations, on the processes of the normalization of artistic behaviors, and on the balance between reproductive inertia and innovation, particularly in the domain of jazz, where innovation is an essential value.

It was thanks especially to Hughes that Becker succeeded, if not yet in answering the question, at least in placing it in the ranks of sociological problems. Hughes's chief area of interest was the sociology of work. His motto was "Everything is somebody's work," "by which he meant that in any complex society, and in most of the activities of less complex societies, all aspects of everyday life result in fact from a specialist's full-time work, and that almost all situations can be understood by studying them from the angle of work."[1]

What Hughes sensed was that some behaviors in "inferior" occupations made it possible to see, much more explicitly than in the most elevated categories, attitudes that were generally shared in work relationships.[2] For example, scorn for those who pay them will be expressed less easily by a lawyer or a doctor than by a household employee or a Saturday night musician. According to Becker, "I was the man he [Hughes] was looking for: the one who was going to study people whose way of organizing work would reveal the processes hidden in other types of activity. So I became his student and learned to see everything as being 'somebody's work.'"

> "Everything" included art, which my own experience as an art worker disposed me to see anyway. If art was work, that meant a quite different approach from the philosophical and historical one then prevalent in the sociology of art. It meant studying how the people who made and distributed and consumed art managed to carry off that complex enterprise with as little trouble as they had. That, in turn, meant concrete studies of the work situations of art production and consumption.[3]

From this point of view, Becker could find practically nothing in the existing sociology of art to base his research on. The then-current sociology of art, with a very few notable exceptions, such as the work of Raymonde Moulin,[4] focused essentially on problems related to aesthetics, the major ambition being to collect criteria that would make it possible to distinguish works belonging to the category of "great art" from the rest. Concerning music, he could obviously not base himself on Adorno, whom he soon ceased to take seriously because of the German author's total blindness regarding jazz and, moreover, other musical and artistic questions in general.

At the time, American sociology being of no more help, he had to construct a sociology without sociological bases. The bases came from elsewhere, such as from practice: that of jazz and the many "Saturday night groups" that Becker had participated in since his student days in Chicago and that of photography, which he learned later on. But he also drew from neighboring disciplines that provided him with the tools he needed to answer the perennial questions. For jazz, he wanted to know how these bands managed to play together and how they managed to stop together. And how did their activity interest anyone at all? How did people recognize art in it, that is, as an activity with some value? And what kind of pleasure did people feel while listening to it?

The Conventional Basis of Artistic Activity

When you read Howard Becker, everything seems simple. He takes particular care to write in a clear style and does not overload his texts with multiple references to works and authors with whom he is nonetheless in dialogue. As a result, his hypotheses, like his results, soon appear familiar to his readers as if they were due mainly to solid, practical good sense. But this should not make us forget either our author's refined culture or the tenacity of his investigative work, which constantly seeks to get behind appearances to avoid overly simple answers slapped onto questions that he has patiently helped make simple.

The vigilance of his investigation takes work. Like a musician, the sociologist has to practice his scales. He has to constantly exercise his gaze and his ability to ask questions. In the course of his career, Becker perfected his sociological scales, and he offers them to us carelessly, without lecturing anyone, under the name of "tricks of the trade." One of the most important of these tricks is of some help for the problem that concerns us here:

> The simplest trick of all is just to insist that nothing that can be imagined is impossible, so we should look for the most unlikely things we can think of and incorporate their existence, or the possibility of their existence, into our thinking.[5]

In other words, as he often says, "things could have happened differently."

Thus, it can be supposed that the musicians' playing might have had no basis, which would lead them to redefine every day not only the conditions of their cooperation but also the very definition of their music and the type of relationship they could have with their environment, with their employers and audiences in particular. Becker likes to cite a real example of behavior very close to this. The composer Harry Partch had decided to use a forty-two-note scale. There were no musical instruments with forty-two notes, so he had to invent and construct them himself.

When the instruments were made, no one knew how to play them, and so he had to teach a generation of Partch instrumentalists. He not only had to teach them to play the instruments but also, because no forty-two-tone notation existed, had to invent the notation and teach them that as well. And since there was no literature for a music based on forty-two tones, he had to write that too (which, of course, was why he had gone to all that trouble in the first place). This music was played in a concert and recorded.

This constitutes one way of escaping from what ordinarily allows us to play music together. There are other possible ways to escape it, but in general neither Partch's nor the others are used because they consume too much time and energy. In fact, it took Partch about nine months to prepare a two-hour concert, whereas an ordinary group devotes six to nine hours to the preparation of such a concert.

What allows us to gain so much time, what usually allows us to play music together, what makes it so that, in general, "things do not happen in a different way," is the crux of the problem. We are forced to note that artistic activity is supported by regular ways of doing things and of experiencing the art that is practiced, regular ways crystallized in the objects used and stabilized in normal behaviors and in habitual relationships among the actors. Becker found a definition of these "musical ways"—these ways of making art, these ways of living together and acting together—in the term "convention" used by various authors, notably musicologists and historians of art.

It was in Leonard Meyer's *Emotion and Meaning in Music* that Becker discovered, with this notion, a way of conceiving of the collective aspect of music. In the conventional ways of organizing sound (scales, chords, cadences), Meyer saw the dynamizing principles of musical experience. According to Becker:

> Put simply, the conventional forms create, in the musician and the listener, expectations as to what will follow, and we thus expect that a note in a chord will follow another note in the same chord. Breaking these conventions, or delaying their conventional resolution, provokes a tension, and the alternation of tension and resolution creates the emotional and intellectual effect of music.[6]

Even in the artistic domain, where the role played by creation and sometimes by improvisation is supposed to be greater than elsewhere, conventions are omnipresent. They dictate the choice of materials, indicate the procedures that will make it possible to convey ideas or elicit emotions, govern forms and artistic genres, "suggest the appropriate dimensions of a work, the proper length of a performance, the proper size and shape of a painting or sculpture. Conventions regulate the relations between artists and audience, specifying the rights and obligations of both."[7]

Conventions are first of all a kind of knowledge constitutive of a particular culture. In a given culture, everyone knows them more or less, because they have learned them through various channels, even if a deeper knowledge of the conventions of a genre, being established as artistic competence, distinguishes well-informed amateurs from laypeople.

This conventional knowledge is a stabilized activity that has agreed upon its procedures, its techniques, and its multiple choices to make cooperation among different actors easier.

> There is no logical reason, for instance, to tune musical instruments to a concert A that is 440 vibrations per second, no reason why that note should be called A instead of Z, and no reason why those notes should be written on a staff of five lines instead of four, six, or seven. But everyone does it that way and thus any one participant can be sure that what he does that way will be intelligible and easy to coordinate with. Reason enough.[8]

Thus, we also find conventions, in a rigidified form, in the material objects we use, which are what they are because they have been stabilized by custom. We find them in the formal organization of activities—for example, the whole set of acts involved in the organization of a concert. But they are also present in the more or less explicitly codified ritual activity that is carried out to satisfy the needs of social exchanges that have no particular goal. And face-to-face relationships, even though they may be unprecedented, not only are based on a whole conventional baggage learned through other encounters and observed in other situations but soon establish their own reference points that will serve as a basis for future exchanges.

The notion of convention has to be understood flexibly. It clearly implies putting restrictions on creative activity, but it also makes possible the exploration of all the possibilities offered within the framework of the rule itself. Thus, in the domain of art, a conventional form does not in any way ensure sterility. It not only authorizes sharing an activity but also requires subtle exploitations of the room for maneuver in and with the rule to obtain effects that are always new, even though they can be shared thanks to their fidelity to the rule. As a result, "we can understand any work of art as the product of a choice between conventional ease and success and unconventional trouble and lack of recognition."[9]

Conventions, therefore, make cooperation possible. But cooperation has to be understood in the strong sense, which covers not only practices—playing a piece of music, building a railroad bridge, or stepping aside to let someone enter the post office— but also representations, feelings, and, in the artistic domain, which is the one where it is a specialty to cultivate them, emotions. Artistic cooperation is not only the kind of cooperation engaged in by members of a jazz group. It is what the musicians and their audiences do together: sharing emotions. Leonard Meyer, like other analysts, saw

> the concept of the artistic convention useful in explaining artists' ability to make art works which evoke an emotional response in audiences. By using such a conventional organization of tones as a scale, composers can create and manipulate listeners' expectations as to what sounds will follow. They can then delay and frustrate the satisfaction of those expectations, generating tension and release as the expectation is ultimately satisfied. Only because artist and audience share knowledge of and experience with the conventions invoked does the art work produce an emotional effect.[10]

Becker found the possibility of taking the notion of convention as foundational confirmed in other authors, though none was a sociologist: Barbara Herrnstein Smith, who applied it to poetry, and Ernst Gombrich, William Ivins, and Michael Baxandall, who applied it to art history.

Armed with a notion of convention envisaged both as a formula of cooperation and as the baggage of emotional education, Becker was able to launch into the elaboration of a sociology of art that from the outset escaped the considerable difficulties experienced by many other sociological approaches to art that proceed on the assumption of a hiatus between each of the three supposed "elements" of artistic activity: production, artwork, reception. Once these are separated, it becomes difficult to reconnect them and to reunify the artistic process. To do so, one has to postulate an encounter, which is rather difficult to define, between the artist's presumed "intention"—or an intention that is supposed to pass through him without his knowing it—and audiences' presumed "receptivity." And this encounter is generally founded on a level other than artistic activity itself, that of overall structures and dynamics, in which the notion of social classes soon resurfaces.

For Becker, artistic activity is already a sharing because it is based on the shared framework of social conventions. Since art thus consists—as do other social activities, but in a special way—in playing among ourselves on the basis of equipment (i.e., conventions) that unites us in advance, all the questions that sociology can address to art remain, but at least art can be questioned in a way different from the way it is questioned in sociologies of separation. Moreover, the goal of Becker's sociology is not necessarily to resolve all the problems that art may raise for sociology. Its major and crucial contribution consists in saying: let's reorient thinking about art as an activity, the notion of convention allowing us to understand the basis on which it can be considered a social activity, and let's see what such a reorientation can produce. It was this new perspective, which is innovative and modest at the same time, that was to lead Becker to establish the notion of "art worlds."

The Artist Multiplied

At the foundation of the methodological proposition covered by the notion of "art worlds" is a resolute rejection of the representation of the artist generally adopted by common sense and carefully maintained by art markets: that of the sovereign artist, the possessor of special gifts, the solitary inventor of inimitable skills who holds a monopoly on authentic creation. The value assigned to artworks is based on the value assigned to this essential figure. This representation of the artist culminated in

> the Romantic myth of the artist, [which] suggests that people with such gifts cannot be subjected to the constraints imposed on other members of society; we must allow them to violate rules of decorum, propriety, and common sense everyone else must follow or risk being punished. The myth suggests that in return society receives work of unique character and invaluable quality.[11]

Only by recognizing this representation is it possible to penetrate art worlds and understand their functioning. There are many ways of doing that, many ways of removing the artist from his pedestal. It has been shown, notably by Michael Baxandall, that this belief has not always existed, that it really developed only in Western societies and only since the Renaissance, which greatly reduces its import. Confining oneself to a very modest critique of the idea of "gift," one can also assemble countless testimonies by artists emphasizing that success in this domain is largely the result of assiduous labor, daily work, at least as much as it is the result of an inexplicable inspiration.[12] One can also show, by an equally modest critique of the "belief" in the value of artworks, that the myth of the artist is a snake that bites its own tail once the works' success depends less on exceptional, immediately visible qualities than on the signature they bear. When famous artists—and Trollope himself tried this experiment—publish works under a borrowed name, they go completely unnoticed. Thus, we are clearly in the presence of a mental construction in which the figure of the artist and the value of the artwork constantly reinforce each other. "The ideology posits a perfect correlation between doing the core activity and being an artist. If you do it, you must be an artist. Conversely, if you are an artist, what you do must be art."[13] To which we can add: if you are a great artist, what you do is necessarily great art, and vice versa.

Thus we see that the angles from which the myth of the artist can be attacked are diverse and have been taught by many specialists, whether they were sociologists or not. However, Becker uses such arguments only incidentally. The fact that the artistic "gift" is a socially and historically constructed ideology does not lead him to deny that there are unequally distributed qualities and that some people more clearly achieve a level of excellence than others. His criticism's target is not artistic excellence (I shall return to his positions with regard to artists' reputations). For him, the essential point is to show that no matter at what their level, all artists need to rely on cooperative chains and that wherever the debates on the points discussed earlier might lead, this fact suffices to require that artistic activity be conceived differently, not as being under the haughty patronage of the sovereign artist. Furthermore, from the very first lines of *Art Worlds*, Becker makes clear his visceral antielitism.[14]

All artists need chains of cooperation. The example of the jazz concert mentioned in the prologue to this book is perhaps too facile, because it refers, essentially, to face-to-face situations in which mutual adaptation for a common production is inevitable. But let us take up briefly the example of a solitary artist, one who is apparently the sole master of his art, asking nothing of anyone and owing nothing to anyone. That is, it seems, the poet's case. His needs are minimal, only a little material. Few people will read him. And he seems authorized to invent a language in which images are deployed with complete freedom.

And yet poetry exists only because it is made available for reading. Actors other than the poet must therefore be involved. There have to be publishers who agree to take the economic risk of publishing this kind of literature, which is said to be read by no one. There have to be distributors, critics, and periodicals that reserve space for poetry; contests have to be organized and prizes awarded. Public poetry readings have to be set up, so actors or poetry lovers have to learn to recite this particular kind of text properly, and readers have to have learned to like reading or listening to verse and to continue to recognize poetry when it is in prose.

Such learning processes are themselves possible only on the basis of poetic conventions. There are fixed forms: the sonnet, the ode, the ballad. There are genres: lyric, epic, satirical, and light poetry. There is a linguistic register: not everything in the linguistic repertory is poetic to the same extent, and introducing into poetry something that was not formerly part of it (e.g., in different periods, slang or the language of hoodlums) is a choice, a daring act that carries a risk. At any given moment, these conventions constitute the stabilized outcome of poetic work. Basing himself on them, even if only to subvert them, every poet writes his work in dialogue with a long series of actors in the world of poetry.

The poet also writes in dialogue with those who are expected to receive his work. Every artist speculates on other people's affective and intellectual reactions to his work.[15] And these anticipated reactions, which fully participate in the ordinary process of interaction, are a determining element of his artistic choices.

The face-to-face relation is thus only a special case of the cooperation necessary for artistic activity. No artist is completely isolated from others' work. Conventions, like the professional organization of an artistic activity, constitute a kind of socially constructed baggage that is stored in the poet's attic, even if he is solitary and would like to think himself condemned.

The analysis of any artistic situation leads to the same conclusion: the possibility of the existence of any work of art is connected to a chain of cooperation involving both persons currently active and past work stabilized in genre conventions:

> All artistic work, like all human activity, involves the joint activity of a number, often a large number, of people. Through their cooperation, the art work we eventually see or hear comes to be and continues to be. The work always shows signs of that cooperation. The forms of cooperation may be ephemeral, but often become more or less routine, producing patterns of collective activity we can call an art world.[16]

Moreover, in certain artistic disciplines—such as the cinema, where the division of labor is particularly complex—it can be difficult to tell "who the artist is" when several specialists claim to be doing the greater part of the work.[17]

The Distribution of Artistic Work

By thus shifting the viewpoint from which sociology can study art, and by ceasing to observe the figure of the artist alone, we have at the same time transformed the object of investigation. What we must henceforth understand by "art" is not only the finished product that proceeds from the artist's mind and hands, that is, the artwork, but also the common activity, the whole set of things that are done by various people so that at the end of conventionally stabilized collective processes, the object that we call an artwork can appear. "The object of our analysis is not the work of art as an isolated reality (an object or manifestation), but rather the whole set of stages of its creation and its re-creation as people discover and enjoy it."[18] I shall return to the significance of this reorientation of the very object of the sociology of art, this relativizing of artworks so that they are no longer the whole of art but only one element produced among others thanks to the set of cooperative operations that constitute an art world. But before doing that, I have to provide a more precise view of what an "art world" is.

The notion of "art world" is far from referring only to the image of it we might find on the society pages: a limited social circle of persons for whom art is a major interest, the small world of artists and art lovers who regularly meet at events intended to bring them together and to make it known that they have met. Even though that is part of it, an art world is based less on this complicity connected with the ostensible sharing of a symbolic power than on acts that are often more modest and less visible, concrete exchanges of services without which no artistic production is possible. "Art worlds consist of all the people whose activities are necessary to the production of the characteristic works that that world, and perhaps others as well, define as art."[19]

Seen from the point of view of its activity, an art world is thus a mobilization around art, around the project of making art, of persons, energies, investments, materials, knowledge, and techniques. In it we note the existence of a limited stock of materials and available actors (at a given time, only certain types of photographic paper are on the market; or we find more guitarists than violinists on the market). These limits simultaneously influence the works that can be produced and make organization of the management and supply of these resources obligatory.

As for its form, an art world is a network whose center is constituted by the place where the artworks are made under the control of those who are usually called artists, and it is organized into multiple chains of cooperation, including the cooperation of "support personnel" who are more or less distant from the places where the final acts of creation take place but whose participation is no less essential to the process. In the case of literature, for example, support personnel include critics, organizers of panel discussions on books that have just come out, and, of course, readers.

When it becomes necessary, for reasons of methodology, to range so far in gathering together those who participate in an art world, we understand that its borders are not clear. For instance, the different art worlds constantly overlap: a literary work may include illustrations and thus call upon another chain of cooperation; a film can be based on a novel. And we can follow the chain of contributions to artistic production very far back: is the inventor of a word-processing program part of the world of literature? Yes, if the program was conceived to solve problems specific to literary publication. As a criterion of delimitation, we can say that art worlds stop where the actors cease to refer to the artistic practice in question, even if they provide services that, albeit in a remote way, are used in that practice.

> Art worlds do not have boundaries around them allowing us to say that these people belong to a particular art world while those people do not. I am not concerned with drawing a line separating an art world from other parts of a society. Instead, we look for groups of people who cooperate to produce things that they, at least, call art; having found them, we look for other people who are also necessary to that production, gradually building up as complete a picture as we can of the entire cooperating network that radiates out from the work in question. The world exists in the cooperative activity of those people.[20]

Everywhere in such a network, at its center as well as at its peripheries, the activity in an art world can and must be regarded as a job. First of all, resources—both material (objects, raw materials, money, places, equipment) and human (lighting engineers, star dancers, builders of picture frames, manufacturers of tubes of paint, lute players, sound recorders)—have to be brought in and made available where they are needed.

The stock on hand and the techniques available for using that stock constitute constraints on artistic activity. However, these limits are constantly subverted, both by developing new materials and by using existing materials in new ways. As for the supply of support personnel, in theory it is characterized by the possibility that artists can find interchangeable personnel at any time. However, they may have to cope with a relative shortage: "There will usually be an oversupply of people for the roles thought to contain some element of the 'artistic'—in theater that includes playwrights, actors, and directors—and a short supply of people with technical skills to do support work that does not share in that charisma."[21] It is important to emphasize the real role played by support personnel. It cannot be seen solely in terms of limits and shortages. A serious sociology of art has to be combined with the sociology of artistic professions and to recognize in them a genuine labor power, which is often organized and whose action actually affects the contents of artworks. Because even if support personnel are said to be "secondary" in the process of creation, they are not subject to the all-powerful decisions of the artist and in no way constitute a simple technical auxiliary. For an artist to get what he wants out of the close relations that he maintains with his support personnel, the latter have to be able to provide support for him; that is, they have to have acquired, in one way or another, the necessary skills. But it is also necessary that the artist want support, that his attention has been caught and his interest aroused, and that performances not be expected of him that are incompatible with his current status and his career perspectives. Thus, it is neither surprising nor abusive that "many members of the support group once performed, or still have the feeling of performing, a genuine artistic activity."[22] Without exaggerating its import, this positive contribution must be stressed, especially since, as Pierre-Michel Menger emphasizes in his preface to the French translation of *Art Worlds*, it radically distinguishes Becker's sociology of art from critical interpretations in the mode of the Frankfurt School, which conceive of the relations between the intermediaries of the market and artists as being for the latter pure situations of dependence, exploitation, and alienation. On the contrary, Becker reminds us that dependence is not conceivable outside a framework of interdependence.[23]

But this in no way implies that the necessary cooperation includes only friendly arrangements and always tends toward conciliation. Conflict is part of art worlds, ordinarily, normally, as in social life in general.

For the moment, we can limit ourselves to this broad definition:

> A "world of art" is constituted by the whole of those whose activities are necessary for the production and the reception of characteristic works of art that this world, and sometimes others as well, defines as art. The actors in these art worlds coordinate operations that lead to the production of the work, referring to a set of shared values that are manifested in common practices and in regularly used artifacts. Often the same actors cooperate in an almost-routine way to produce similar works, so that we can consider a "world of art" as an established network of links of cooperation among the actors. Works of art are not the product of brilliant individuals but rather the collective result of the work of all those who cooperate through the conventions characteristic of a world of art that make it possible for these works to exist.[24]

What Is the Value of Artworks Based On?

Here we are not dealing solely with a "utilitarian" approach to art that aims to give an account of the conditions of the possibility of its material and organizational functioning. The notion of "art worlds" also asserts its pertinence regarding properly aesthetic questions and allows us to formulate an analytical perspective on the question of the value of art.

The main problem raised by aestheticians concerns what can be rightly designated as art and what cannot. From Becker's viewpoint, we should stop considering aesthetics to be a lofty discipline that looks down on the world of art from on high and formulates judgments about works in themselves, independently of the conditions under which artistic activity is carried out. On the contrary, aesthetics itself can be seen as an activity, one of the forms of activity developed by art worlds.

Aesthetics is not pure thought. It is a product of judgments, values, and reputations on which transactions, speculations, investments, and thus various kinds of remuneration are based. Aestheticians seek to construct systems to classify things and define what beauty is, what art is, etc. Critics use these systems to formulate judgments that confer value on works. From this arises the reputation of works and artists. And naturally the market is dependent on this scale of values.

Aesthetics is an activity shared by participants in art worlds. To be sure, it has its specialists (philosophers, professional critics), but in a world of art, everyone is constantly making aesthetic judgments. The question is what criteria these judgments are based on. Is there an essence of art the knowledge of which would ensure that critics and philosophers can make reliable classifications? At the opposite extreme, does art proceed from self-proclamation, as certain works that inaugurated contemporary art (those of Duchamp, in particular) might suggest?

Observation of the facts hardly confirms either of these interpretations. Nowhere do we find a clear distinction between art and non-art. If we drew up a list of criteria for defining what constitutes art, they would almost never all be present in objects that are nonetheless recognized as art. However, self-proclamation cannot suffice either; entry into networks of distribution that accept the self-proclaimed artwork is also necessary. Finally, everything cannot be art for a practical reason: there is not enough room in museums for so many additional works, not enough room in cities for so many additional museums, etc. There is not enough room on radio schedules or on the racks of specialized music stores for many more pop singers than there already are.

These considerations, which appear down-to-earth, lead us to connect aesthetic judgment with the organization of art worlds. Following this path, Becker found support, or in any case intuitions, in what is known as institutional aesthetic theory, particularly in the work of George Dickie and Arthur Danto; the latter had already used the term "art worlds." These authors recognized the reality of the organization of art worlds and its importance for the formulation of aesthetic judgments, but it was a merely theoretical recognition. Danto does speak of "art worlds," but for him they are only a kind of support, something that could be used to talk about specific works, but does not do so in his analysis. Moreover, both Dickie and Danto continue to seek a principle that distinguishes between art and non-art.

Becker's position on this subject is that of a relativist sociologist:

> We see, too, that in principle any object or action can be legitimated as art, but that in practice every art world has procedures and rules governing legitimation which, while not clear-cut or foolproof, nevertheless make the success of some candidates for the status of art very unlikely. Those procedures and rules are contained in the conventions and patterns of cooperation by which art worlds carry on their routine activities.[25]

Thus, there is no absolute artistic value but only relative values that are conferred by organized social milieus. There is no inherent value in works but only values on which it has been possible to agree. The condition of the possibility of artistic value is consensus within an art world:

> judgments of value not held jointly by members of an art world do not provide a basis for collective activity premised on those judgments, and thus do not affect activities very much. Work becomes good, therefore valuable, through the achievement of consensus about the basis on which it is to be judged and through the application of the agreed-on aesthetic principles to particular cases.[26]

The origin of such a consensus can reside only in the common interactions that make an art world exist. And the sociology of art thus finds itself regularly sent back to its obligations to make on-site observations by going to see "who actually does what with whom."[27]

Making the Artwork Uncertain

Becker's sociology of art does not call upon works of art to rescue an overall sociology and does not seek to accord them interest because of their ability to interpret the world, to express the profound reasons it has to be what it is, or to anticipate what it might or ought to be. It raises the problem of artworks at another, apparently more modest level, that of an occupational sociology, by showing what tools those who undertake to make art can provide themselves with to organize an effective network in this domain. This network is effective on different levels: it organizes activities; distributes art's materials and workers; stabilizes procedures, techniques, and conventional representations; organizes artists' careers and support personnel's careers; and serves, finally, as the instrument for regulating the distribution of value to things having to do with art.

Contrary to the objections that have sometimes been made to this sociology,[28] the question of artworks is present in it. But we must take care, with Becker, to define clearly what we mean by "artwork" and to understand the way in which his studies radically renew the sociological approach to artworks.

Becker urges us to reconsider the customary point of view according to which the artist and the work are the central elements, distributing value and meaning to everything that is done within artistic systems. We have already seen how it was judicious to consider such systems from another angle by ceasing to organize them around the sovereign figure of the artist and by understanding their activity as that of complex networks of cooperation. The same path must be followed with respect to artworks.

The same common opinion maintains that artworks are the point of departure for operations of classification through which great art is distinguished from expressions of lesser value. It is usually thought that artists' reputations are based on works. A "theory of reputation" has thus been established:

1) Specially gifted people 2) create works of exceptional beauty and depth which 3) express profound human emotions and cultural

values. 4) The work's special qualities testify to its maker's special gifts, and the already known gifts of the maker testify to the special qualities of the work. 5) Since the works reveal the maker's essential qualities and worth, all the works that person makes, but no others, should be included in the corpus on which his reputation is based.[29]

Becker reorients this point of view by showing that the common representation of the work and the artist is illusory insofar as it imagines art worlds as having as their sole purpose to distinguish the conditions for the pure autonomy of the creative act. It is as if the only function of the support personnel is to help the artist be alone with his work, which is assumed to arise from a pure contact with essential values. All Becker's work has consisted, on the contrary, in establishing the complete solidarity of the activities operating in a world of art. The value of the works, their reputation and that of the artists, does not proceed from a private and solitary relationship with Beauty, the Sublime, or whatever it might be, detached from the occupational activities that led to their birth, from the organization of those activities, and from the type of problem resolution that making them entailed. It is not the works that regulate one another in a purely aesthetic operation; rather, it is the forms taken by artistic cooperation that cause the works to be classified in categories such as great art, popular art, etc.:

> Wherever an art world exists, it defines the boundaries of acceptable art, recognizing those who produce the work it can assimilate as artists entitled to full membership, and denying membership and its benefits to those whose work it cannot assimilate. If we look at things from a commonsense point of view, we can see that such large-scale editorial choices made by the organizations of an art world exclude many people whose work closely resembles work accepted as art. We can see, too, that art worlds frequently incorporate at a later date works they originally rejected, so that the distinction must lie not in the work but in the ability of an art world to accept it and its maker.[30]

Or again, expressed more concisely, "it is art worlds rather than artists that make works of art."[31]

The typology of artists presented in *Art Worlds*,[32] which ranges from the integrated professional to the amateur, via freelancers and popular artists, designates something other than processes of exclusion based solely on the works created, and also something other than persons and profiles of artists: it designates more or less eccentric modes of work in a world of art, relations that people maintain with a world of art, and careers that usually lead to the production of works that will be received in different ways, are visible in places that are generally unaware of each other, and are honored in unequal ways. Of course, all this cannot exclude either reevaluations of genres (a sudden overevaluation of the popular, for instance) or changes in the careers of artists or of other members of the art world. As I shall have occasion to emphasize again because it is an essential characteristic, Becker's sociology is fundamentally flexible, holding that everyone can always act differently—in short, that everything is possible.

However, although everything is possible, everything has a price. Every choice made constitutes a change in a career's direction, at the cost of a certain recognition or a certain exclusion. It is in these itineraries in the art worlds, and in all the interactions between their regular forms and each individual's capacity for action and initiative—interactions that constantly redefine art worlds—that works are produced and reputations defined at the same time, the reputations of artists, genres, disciplines, and the works themselves.

What can finally be defined as "the work itself"? For Becker, nothing is added to the qualification of the work by adding "itself." Formulating things in that way generally means: let's take an interest only in the final result—the picture, the novel—since after all (and this is what is really included in the little word "itself") it is the only thing that is meaningful. This is a temptation frequently encountered by sociologists of art. But what is meaningful is not only the picture, or whatever it is. Becker's whole sociology seeks to say that the picture is the product of a collective activity that in the course of its execution has involved choices made by a very large number of people performing different functions all through the process of its construction.

Moreover, if it is thus reduced to itself, the work generally cannot be found. What picture are we talking about, or which play? A painter usually makes multiple preliminary sketches, ways of approaching his subject. Which of these is the one that has the most "meaning"? The one that finally hangs on the wall in the museum? It is clear that if we choose that one, we are basing its additional meaning on something other than the work itself: namely, on the labor and the choices of those who have designated this picture, rather than others very close to it and almost identical with it, to appear in the museum. And what are we to say about a play? Is it the canonical text, *ne varietur*, that appears in the definitive edition of an author's works? But theater is not solely a text; it is a production and an interpretation. Plays that continue to be part of the artistic heritage are staged in many different ways, and in each of them the interpretation changes in the course of the performances. Which is the right one? The role of the sociologist of art is to give an account—also—of the work of choosing incumbent on certain people who define what "the work in itself" is, but he cannot substitute himself for them. For his part, he must recall that the work was produced by everyone all along the chain, and that it is the final result of the whole set of choices that have been made all along that chain. Thus, Becker ultimately formulates the "principle of the fundamental indetermination of the work of art":

> That is, it is impossible, in principle, for sociologists or anyone else to speak of the "work itself" because there is no such thing. There are only the many occasions on which a work appears or is performed or is viewed, each of which can be different from all the others.[33]

This in no way means merely that the sociologist has to consider the work to be deprived of meaning. If, on the contrary, it is full of meaning, that is because one of the aspects of the conventional activity of art worlds consists in overloading it with meaning. And this activity is carried out within the frameworks of artistic experience that are called conventions and in the constant redefinition of or a certain play with those conventions. And critics and audiences will in turn do their work of endowing the work with meaning, joining in the play with the conventions in force. Beckerian sociology is a sociology of works of art, but it is an open sociology: it asks neither sociologists nor works to establish the meaning of the latter, to define their message. Neither does it presuppose that works bear meaning, because they can also elicit pure emotive pleasure, simple complicity with forms that have no need to be enrolled in the order of the word, of commentary, of the philosophy of art. And when it happens that they are loaded with such words, Becker's sociology limits itself to observing their sociological distribution, to considering the actions of those whose occupation is to make works speak, an occupation that is neither more nor less interesting than all the others, than all the occupations that are concerned with "making art" and that, taken together, "make a work." It is all these activities that are constantly opening and closing, only to open once again, the meanings of the work.

This extract from a letter to Charles Seeger, the famous ethnomusicologist, sums up the basic orientation Becker gives to the sociology of art:

> I have in mind instead a discipline which is really a subfield of empirical sociology, in which the emphasis is on occupational organization, the development and maintenance of traditions, the training of practitioners, mechanisms of distribution, and audiences and their tastes. The basic imagery in this kind of sociology is of art as something people do together. Sociologists working in this mode aren't much interested in "decoding" artworks, in finding the works' secret meanings as reflections of society. They prefer to see those works as the result of what a lot of people have done jointly. While the imagery of the older sociology of art emphasizes great geniuses working more or less in isolation—the studies are of great novelists or composers—the imagery underlying this other version is more likely to be drawn from one of the collective arts, like filmmaking, where it might even be hard to tell who to credit or blame for the work you see. This sociology of art is less interested in genius and in rare works and more interested in journeymen and routine work, which, of course, most art consists of.[34]

3

Culture in Motion

Concepts like "convention" and "world" are inherently general. The last page of *Art Worlds* asks us to make use of them regarding every event in any domain of sociology where networks organize the cooperation of their participants in a regular or routine way.[1] That amounts to asking us to use them very broadly in the framework of a general sociology. Becker notes, moreover, that these tools are very close to those commonly used by diverse sociological traditions:

> I was excited by the idea of "convention" because I could immediately translate it into a fundamental idea in the sociological study of collective activity, which is known under a variety of names: norms, rules, culture, or (my favorite) shared understandings. Or even, one could say, "consensus."[2]

All the same, these concepts concern a very general range of problems: on what do we rely to ensure that the behaviors of different people cohere to do what we have to do together? In other words, what is culture made of? Becker's interactionist model has to be very specific about what distinguishes it from the approaches in other sociological traditions that emphasize "regularities of collective action." What representation of culture can we give ourselves?

Norms and Their Actors

The words "culture," "norms," and "conventions" thus refer to an order of facts, to what makes it possible to establish cooperation and to expect a certain regularity in the accomplishment of acts that have to be undertaken collectively. Becker indicates that in developing his own use of the notion of convention, he relied on the theories of Herbert Blumer, and he describes the general orientation this way:

> People can act together to do whatever they do because they understand what the others involved are likely to do, and so can adjust what they do so that it will fit in. Everyone is engaged in this process of guessing what others will do and adjusting their behavior accordingly, and in this way a kind of shared understanding develops: of what is being done, how it ought to be done, what result it will likely have, and so on.[3]

In this way Becker adopts an approach to culture that is radically different from those of many theories that can be described as sociologies of exteriority and imposition. Without embarking on a detailed critique of the latter, which we find expressed particularly in France in a tradition that runs from Durkheim to Bourdieu, let us simply recall that the norm is seen as external to individuals, and that it belongs to an order of its own that is called "social fact" or "social structure." This order of the collective is imposed on individuals and is unaffected by individual efforts to evade it. In general, individuals conform to it because of varying proportions of authoritarian imposition and interiorization (the incorporation of constraint), by means of which they end up desiring to do what it is "objectively" foreseeable that they will do.

Such conceptions obviously include, as an element that poses a problem, the possibility of change: it is the continuation of normative systems that is predictable and plausible. And deviation from the norm may be manifested, as in Durkheim's theory of anomie, in unhappy or "pathological" behavior.

What emerges, on the contrary, from the sociology exemplified by Howard Becker is a methodological reluctance to accord an operational capacity to abstractions. Neither the norm nor the "social fact" nor the "social structure" nor even convention is a practical reality. The question is always: who is behind the abstraction, who takes responsibility for it, who makes it operational? For something to exist, there has to be someone who is concerned with it. We have seen how works of art exist only so long as they continue to be honored by someone looking at them, interpreting them, commenting on them. For constraining norms to exist, there have to be moral entrepreneurs. It is not enough for a right to exist; it has to be activated, sustained, made use of, and constantly readapted to the circumstances. It is not enough that there be customs, traditions, and collective habits; they have to be maintained, they have to elicit adhesion or rejection, and, in either case, practices have to be developed to do that.

To understand the norm, we have to avoid placing it in an abstract setting; we have to observe it insofar as it is based on an actual agreement. This in no way means that everyone obeys it, because then there would no longer be outsiders and cultural change would be literally impossible; instead, it means only that at a given time everyone can know what behaviors are considered acceptable. Then everything is possible: the normal play of society involves transgressing, discussing, reorienting, and negotiating new arrangements, which all lead to the possibility, or the necessity, of inventing innovative practices.

Thus, norms are not something that preexists, having been established through the play of social forces that by their nature escape our control, and to whose negotiation individuals have little or no access; instead, they are arrangements worked out in the activity and interaction of individuals.

The Interactive Source of Culture

Culture cannot be defined as a preestablished set of tools that shape behaviors and make them coherent. Culture is not a kind of baggage inside us that loads us with ways of doing things, thinking, and feeling that are peculiar to the group to which we belong. That kind of baggage is generally supposed to instill in us dispositions that prepare us to react in certain ways in our encounters with others and with the world.

The interactionist approach essentially does away with this idea of cultural baggage, or in any case transforms it. Above all, it ceases to reason as though culture existed before the real life of each of us, as if each group provided for each of its members an identity that precedes any confrontation with others. On the contrary, what characterizes culture, first of all, is the fact that it is an activity. Different people's activities intersect on a common terrain and become mutually comprehensible, and in this way the conditions for the coordination of people's actions emerge. Thus, culture is not essentially something extraindividual, something we receive from the outside—precepts, demands, customs, and rules—and that we absorb in order to transform it into dispositions to act in one way or another. On the contrary, it is born in the dynamic of interindividual relations; culture precedes individual strategies toward others. Thus, we must see culture as a process: it is the creation, in interaction, of the conditions of the possibility of harmonizing behaviors.

These conditions of possibility are what Becker calls "shared understandings":

> People have ideas about how a certain type of activity might be carried out. They believe others share these ideas and one thinks that everyone will act on them if they understand the situation in the same way. They believe further that the people they are interacting with believe that they share those ideas too, so everyone thinks that everyone else has the same idea about how to do things. Given such circumstances, if everyone does what seems appropriate, action will be sufficiently coordinated for practical purposes. Whatever was under way will get done—the meal served, the child dealt with, the job finished—all well enough so that life can proceed.[4]

Thus, we have here a dynamic and extremely flexible conception of culture. Culture is the trajectory of action in which action is constantly influenced by exploratory vigilance—accounted for by the notions of "reflexivity" and "analysis of the situation"—and presupposes its ability to cohere with the actions of others. Culture is constructed "in situations," and the result ordinarily expected—the successful accomplishment of an action performed together—is constructed in the course of the cultural process.

Although it is flexible, such a conception of culture plays out in complicated ways. For one thing, it isn't likely that different people's understandings of a situation converge without trouble of some kind. Life situations, especially in complex societies, never cease to create unprecedented problems:

> Since no two situations are alike, the cultural solutions available for them are only approximate. Even in the simpler societies, no two people learn quite the same cultural material; the chance encounters of daily life provide sufficient variation to preclude that. No set of cultural understandings, then, provides a perfectly applicable solution to any problem people have to solve in the course of their day, and they therefore must remake those solutions, adapt their understandings to the new situation in the light of what is different about it.[5]

This argument merely reinforces the thesis that "individuals never cease to create culture."[6] Nevertheless, we have to take into account that we are not constantly inventing the whole set of behaviors and modes of organization that we adopt. Although it has to constantly invent, culture also endows itself with regular responses endorsed by custom and by the satisfaction they provide. We know that this is the meaning of the idea of convention. Must it be repeated that conventions are forms of action that are not given but constructed, that behind them are the men and women who conceived and established them? Becker takes the concrete example of the everyday action of doing the shopping. It is certain that the second half of the twentieth century witnessed a profound transformation of behaviors in this domain. Small stores became increasingly rare and were replaced by supermarkets. The presentation of commodities changed and so did the ways of supplying them. All this may be related to general social structures and to the evolution of global capitalism, but it is nonetheless true that it is not at the level of such abstractions that we must seek the cause of the cultural transformations in this domain. The concept of a supermarket was created by actual individuals, real people who imagined new systems of collecting and distributing merchandise. And concrete men and women had, in turn, to invent new ways of doing their shopping.[7] We thus remain in the logic of cultural creation.

But we also have to take into account the fact that conventions ensure a certain stability, that they are reproduced by groups of people who did not invent them themselves. We must then incorporate relative stability into the definition of culture and recognize that culture in actuality also includes given elements that preexist a concrete action and are reproducible and often reproduced,[8] though they are constantly revised:

> There is an apparent paradox here. On the one hand, culture persists and antedates the participation of particular people in it; indeed, culture can be said to shape the outlooks of people who participate in it. But cultural understandings, on the other hand, have to be reviewed and remade continually, and in the remaking they change.[9]

The objection that culture is given, or received, thus cannot put in question the perspective of culture as continually being created collectively. Interactive relations work with what they have: an individual capacity, an analysis of the situation, an anticipation of shareable understandings, and an available stock of forms of cooperation that are stabilizable, stabilized, and constantly being destabilized:

> To summarize, how culture works as a guide in organizing collective action and how it comes into being are really the same process. In both cases, people pay attention to what other people are doing and, in an attempt to mesh with what they do with those others, refer to what they know (or think they know) in common. So culture is always being made, changing more or less, acting as a point of reference for people engaged in interaction.[10]

Culture in Actuality

Robert Redfield defined culture this way:

> In speaking of "culture," we have reference to the conventional un-
> derstandings, manifest in act and artifact, that characterize societies.
> The "understandings" are the meanings attached to acts and objects.
> The meanings are conventional, and therefore cultural in so far as
> they have become typical for the members of that society by reason
> of inter-communication among the members. A culture is, then, an
> abstraction: it is the type toward which the meanings that the same
> act or object has for the different members of the society tend to
> conform. The meanings are expressed in action and in the results
> of action, from which we infer them; so we may as well identify
> "culture" with the extent to which the conventionalized behavior of
> members of the society is for all the same.[11]

Becker works in the same spirit, seeking what allows actors whose
representations of the situation are more or less shared to cooperate, since they can anticipate the reactions to the same situation of others who are also looking for the shared (symbolic)
meanings conventionally attached to facts and things. But we
still have to be more precise as to what these "representations" or
"shared understandings" are in practice.

To illustrate, let us take once again the example of the Saturday night musicians with whom Becker spent so much time,
dance musicians and jazzmen. Their particular situation at the
time when he was getting ready to write *Outsiders*—their relative
marginality, their not very conformist style, and their participation in activities considered deviant—led him to use the term
"subculture" with reference to them. This is an expression that
he has now ceased to use, maintaining that cultural processes,
the work of culture, are everywhere of the same type, and that
accordingly there are no grounds for distinguishing between cultures in the full sense of the term and cultures that are supposed
to be more furtive or incomplete, partially unachieved, and perhaps less legitimate.[12]

Dance musicians are in fact united by a culture, in the sense that Redfield gave to this term: there exists between them an agreement on conventional ideas, an agreement that provides a shared meaning attributed to actions and things. Such meanings are very typical of the milieus of dance musicians and are established and reinforced through their interactions and serve as a foreseeable support for future actions. This culture is constructed around the following three elements:

— A common activity, with which specific problems are connected;
— A system of representations or, to use an equivalent term, "an organized set of meanings";
— A code of behavior.

The essential occupational problem confronted by dance musicians in 1950s Chicago derived from their status as independent workers who were, as such, subject to two contradictory requirements: that, precisely, of independence, which was particularly valued in the artistic domain, and that of the economic profitability of their activity, which depended on submission to the occupational demands of their customers and employers. All service occupations experience this influence of the customer, who naturally thinks that the price he is paying authorizes him to direct the work and to obtain the kind of product he himself has defined. Jazz music was caught in this dilemma. Chosen for and defined by its virtue of independence (jazz is "that music which is produced without reference to the demands of outsiders"),[13] it was greatly prized by jazz musicians as the only desirable music, the only kind worth playing. At the same time, it was not much appreciated by the public, which preferred more easily identifiable forms of music that were currently associated with the places and circumstances in which the public wanted band music.[14] The occupation of playing jazz was thus a challenge: somehow one had to manage to make a living from one's art by playing the only music one wanted to play, even though the customers who owned the dance halls, the organizers of parties, and the listeners themselves rejected it or tolerated it only as a marginal musical interlude.

Other, easier careers were open to these musicians: "to achieve success [the average musician] finds it necessary to 'go commercial,' that is, to play in accord with the wishes of the nonmusicians for whom he works; in doing so he sacrifices the respect of other musicians and thus, in most cases, his self-respect."[15]

Thus, jazz becomes a symbolic object on the basis of which all the classifications are constructed and the system of dance musicians' representations is elaborated. In it we find an overevaluation of the jazz musician. "The musician is conceived of as an artist who has a mysterious artistic gift setting him apart from all other people. Possessing this gift, he should be free from control by outsiders who lack it. The gift is something which cannot be acquired through education; the outsider, therefore, can never become a member of the group."[16] This feeling of superiority based on a radical, native otherness obviously leads to developing a no-less-radical rejection of any supervision, in particular supervision proceeding from people outside the musical milieu. Becker's investigation provides stupefying examples of the feeling of absolute superiority conferred on the musician, as can be seen in these remarks made by a young musician: "You learn too much being a musician. I mean, you see so many things and get such a broad outlook on life that the average person just doesn't have."[17] Such a vast break can lead only to a division of the world on the basis of the sole category of the ability to appreciate jazz. Thus, there are two kinds of people: jazzmen, whose incredible abilities have just been mentioned, and the rest. In the usual language of jazz musicians, one word suffices to designate all the rest: "squares." Both substantive and objective, designating people and their behaviors, the term "square" can be expanded to include various contents; it refers to everything one doesn't like, to a whole world hostile to and threatening true music, to an insidious army of people without gifts or taste but who are, unfortunately, the ones who pay for it all.

To confront these challenges and to keep the distinction sharp and the musicians' integrity safe, a code of behavior has to be established that combines internal solidarity and resistance to the external threat. A musician does not have the right to criticize another musician or to try to influence him while he is playing. As much as possible, musicians have to develop unconventional ways of life and distinguish themselves from outsiders. "Behavior which flouts conventional social norms is greatly admired."[18] In short, a whole culture is based on what is both a definitive certainty and a project that has constantly to be pursued: "being different," a project that requires self-segregation.

This imaginary confrontation to which the world is supposed to be prey—like the set of procedures through which the impossible distinction between "the sacred and the profane" in the practice of jazz is played out, as well as the negotiating moves of all kinds through which the passion for jazz and the foreignness of the world with respect to it are reconciled, more or less, and always temporarily—emphasizes that Becker's sociology is in no way a pacified representation of social worlds. Neither the real and imaginary conflicts that are present and active in his sociology nor the term of cooperation, no matter how essential it may be, can erase them. Although from a general point of view the idea of a "world" implies the necessary cooperation between musicians and audiences that allows jazz to be played, allows it to exist, it nonetheless remains true that everywhere and always, even in the concert hall where so many musicians try to construct symbolic places of refuge that guarantee noncontamination by the outside world, which includes their own audience and which is sometimes seen as uncultured and threatening, the necessary cooperation is accompanied not only by complicity, shared emotions, and sometimes unique moments of collective fusion but also by distances, separations, and conflict. This remark obviously also holds for any social situation: cooperation is not the antithesis of conflict. It is the necessary framework without which nothing takes place and exists in all the forms that are always and everywhere available to social life.

The Interactionist Perspective

To account for, or at least to illustrate, a number of situations in collective life, the metaphor of chess is tempting. We think first of two players confronting one another and the elaboration of their strategies. They know, obviously, that each move of one of their pieces creates a new situation and that it offers the opponent a certain number of possibilities. The whole art of chess consists in anticipating what the opponent's response will be and, by constructing a strategy extending over several subsequent moves, offering him no more than a minimum of openings for his own strategies. But everybody knows that the game cannot be won at every move, but only at the final point where one checkmates the opponent's king. During the game, one has to accept making sacrifices, one has to create lures and offer the opponent the opportunity to plunge into what one thinks will be dead ends for him.

It may seem that social life can be summed up in the chess game: a situation in which people do something together, with a similar respect for established rules (norms, conventions), with divergent interests (here clearly opposed), each act creating new situations, each player analyzing the situation every time and gauging the opponent's foreseeable responses to his own moves, and finally adjusting what he is doing to include new information provided by the other's reactions.[19]

However, even in the simple image of the chess game, the face-to-face relationship so magisterially studied by Erving Goffman is not the only one involved. Each player interacts with other persons who are also involved in the game, even if they do not have the power to determine directly the bishop's diagonal trajectory, the rook's lateral mobility, or the queen's subtle defense. The chess player has already played other games, he has accumulated a "professional" knowledge, he will have other adversaries in the future, and each of his moves depends on moves already made and moves to come, just as they depend to a certain extent on the fact of playing in a particular place with an audience or not, in a championship match or a simple game between friends, spied upon or not by future opponents. A basic sociological reflex is to constantly expand the definition of the situation, by keeping in mind the idea of a "world":

Obviously, there are never only two people involved. The actor never thinks solely of one person sitting on the other side of the chessboard. Instead, the actor takes into account all the people involved in the action undertaken. Even in a chess game, there are spectators, other players who are potential opponents on other days, the officials of chess societies, family members, etc. In elaborating his strategy, the actor takes into account more or less simultaneously the potential responses of all these people.[20]

The image of the chess game must not lead us to overestimate how much each actor can control the way the collective action takes place. Even chess players make mistakes and anticipate reactions on the part of the opponent that the latter has not considered or has abandoned in the course of the game. A fortiori, in a more extensive situation the role of error, the unforeseen, and the unforeseeable is important. It not only forces constant readjustments; it also makes collective action something that is largely beyond the control of individual strategies. However, it escapes their control in a way different from the one defended by theories of the exteriority of the social fact. Here it is we ourselves who make the social fact: it is not imposed on us from the outside. But what it becomes, at the end of a complex interplay of the expectations and investments of each actor, is hardly foreseeable. On this point, Becker refers to David Mamet's minute analyses of theatrical situations, suggesting that

> in a play, every character in a scene is there for a reason; they are all there to obtain what they want, to achieve what they want to achieve. If they had no reason to be there, they wouldn't be there. For each of them the scene consists in seeking what they are trying to obtain, but for that they have to come to terms with other persons present who are all doing the same thing. The outcome, and the end of the scene, is very likely to be something that none of them wanted. That is what emerges from each one's pursuit of his own goals.[21]

Even if stability and regularity are present in human actions because conventions have been established and because they operate to make reciprocal expectations compatible, we also have to expect the always-possible emergence of the unprecedented, the continual creation of unknown collective situations. Saying that social life is a mixture of effective conventions and the creation of new situations does not contribute much to the debate. It is up to every sociological study to examine concretely this play of "conservatism" and "innovation," the latter being made possible by the fact that collective situations that disconnect themselves from multiple interactions always escape, to a greater or lesser degree, the control of anything at all by anyone at all. Each time, it is important, for each particular situation, to study the multiple ways in which conventions may be only partly efficacious and may be partly foiled and subverted by collective practice. And it is also important to understand how behavior can be readjusted to face up to the unknown and how new situations generate re-analysis and new strategies.

4

A Sociological Perspective

A Sociology of Situations

Howard Becker's sociology (and I mean by that neither a conceptual apparatus nor a theory but rather a procedure or a perspective: how Becker goes about doing sociology) finds its special
object in situations. As we shall see later on, it does not deny itself
a certain exercise of generalization, and it does not reject a priori
any of the available methods, neither a statistical method nor any
other, but instead accords particular value to direct observation
guided by a certain orientation of the sociological way of seeing
things and concrete situations in collective life. I have already
cited Becker's reference to Blumer, who said that sociological
work started with representations of realities collectively experienced and, from them, constructed new representations that
often aimed to be broader and always strove to be more rigorous
and more lucid. The sociological way of seeing things, in its work
of transforming representations, constructs itself and asserts itself
through procedures that are techniques of investigation, techniques of sociological intelligence, to which Becker gives the
modest name "tricks of the trade." The modesty emphasizes the
fact that in reality we have no method that, by itself, is able to
reveal the truth of social life. We have, if we take care to cultivate

them, only tricks that allow us to rid ourselves of conventional representations, to look at reality with new or more curious eyes, and to try to see things that we would not otherwise have seen. But it is always only a question of trying things out, of "seeing what happens" when one uses this or that trick, of gauging the possibility, of reorienting our gaze in such a way as to have something interesting to say.

Let us repeat that this kind of gaze, cultivated by Becker under the guidance of many others and, above all, Herbert Blumer and Everett Hughes, does not lead to saying: here's what the social is; here's what the nature of collective experience is; here's what the key concepts on which one can build a general theory are. Instead, he seeks to provide results of smaller scope, which can be summed up this way: doesn't the fact of reorienting the way in which one generally sees things, of trying to see them differently, open up prospects for a more complete understanding?

Such a question obviously does not contribute much to the debate if we do not define what is meant by "more complete understanding." To do that we have to go a bit farther than Blumer, who never ceased drawing attention, in an obsessive way, to the underlying representations with which sociologists approach the phenomena they study[1] but who never pursued his reflection to the point of finding specific remedies for this.[2] It takes us nowhere, as Blumer thought, to consider negligible the fact that our participation in the collective life of sociological researchers leads us to plaster onto reality ready-made representations (including concepts). On the other hand, we have to recognize that we cannot achieve a complete knowledge of any social fact. Consequently, our work requires us to fill the gaps in our empirical knowledge. And to that end we invent, we elaborate, as a novelist quite legitimately does, a plausible "story." The idea of a "more complete understanding" is nothing but the hypothesis that if, at the cost of a certain training of our gaze and our thought, we try to "change the story," we will give ourselves some chance of constructing a new story that could include more facts or that could provide us with a more subtle understanding of the facts that it contains, notably the choices that actors make in the course of their social itineraries.

"Not accepting a story" means believing that the story's imagery of how this thing really works is wrong in some important way—we can't understand it or we know that it's not true because some facts inconveniently refuse to be congruent with it. When that happens, and we can't elude or finesse it, we try to change the story.[3]

We have seen Becker repeatedly change his story: for instance, when he gave up the notion that deviants—marijuana smokers or others—had inherent psychological characteristics that pre-destined them to engage in such practices, maintaining instead that the stages in a career of deviance led them, by not making choices that might have led them down other paths, to accept a label that others defined for them; or again, when he stopped see-ing artists and art objects as self-creations due to the mysterious distribution of genius and instead maintained that art as a whole was a work process and that artistic conventions were a fabric that interwove decisions made by many modest participants.

Let me further emphasize two remarkable reorientations of the sociological gaze brought about by Howard Becker. The first consists in shifting attention from categories of people to cat-egories of activities. Sociology has an old reflex to treat cohorts of people by dividing them up depending on their social class, their ethnic origin, their gender, their level of education, or any other criterion that would make it possible to differentiate types of people in accord with the needs of each particular study. The hypothesis is always that membership in one or the other of these categories, or placement at the intersection of several of them, can reveal behaviors that are significantly different from those that belong to another category. Becker's objection to this way of proceeding is that it is obliged, by its method, to postulate a coherence, a homogeneity, in people's behavior according to the type by which they are identified. But "it's easily observed that no one ever acts completely in character, just like their type. Every-one's activity is always more various and unexpected than that."[4]

Here we have a simple empirical observation that has no need to be based on some preconception of human freedom. It suffices to recognize that the kind of fashioning by a psychological or sociological type is constantly subjected to the test of change: "Taking everything into consideration, people do whatever they have to or whatever seems good to them at the time, and . . . since situations change, there's no reason to expect that they'll act in consistent ways."[5] One possible solution to this problem (a solution that by no means proceeds from the desire to deny completely the usefulness of sociological types for evaluating regularities of collective life, but that seeks only to define lived experiences more closely) consists in ceasing to see types of people as a unit of observation and examining the types of activity instead. It is reasonable to assume that

> activities will be responses to particular situations, and that the relations between situations and activities will have a consistency that permits generalization, so that you can say something like this: people who are in a situation of kind X, with these kinds of pressures, and these possibilities of action to choose from, will do this. Or you might be able to say that a certain sequence of situations constitutes a pathway likely to be followed by people who have done the thing you're interested in.[6]

Becker built this "trick of the trade" on the work of Alfred Lindesmith. In his studies on opium addiction, Lindesmith had not presupposed that there were types of people who were more likely to become opium addicts. On the contrary, his hypothesis was that certain addictive behaviors could be discerned that people might engage in under certain circumstances. *Outsiders* took the same view. Even if, using a shortcut, Becker sometimes talked about "marijuana users," his interest was clearly centered on the stages in an itinerary, on the new activities that might be offered to a person—such as becoming a regular smoker—when certain stages had been completed. Each time that a new situation emerges in this way, the actors proceed to analyze it and determine the diverse possibilities among which they can choose. For certain categories of people, deviance may well appear as a (more or less precise) statistical promise. We achieve a more complete understanding by taking a type of activity as the privileged object of investigation and observing its characteristic steps, the ones in which other people's reactions reinforce that behavior or not.

Choosing to study primarily activities also has the advantage of making a study more permeable to change:

> Typing people is a way of accounting for regularity in people's actions; typing situations and lines of activity is a different way. Focusing on activities rather than people nudges you into an interest in change rather than stability, in ideas of process rather than structure. You see change as the normal condition of social life, so that the scientific problem becomes not accounting for change or the lack of it, but accounting for the direction it takes, regarding as a special case the situation in which things actually stay the same for a while.[7]

The second notable reorientation, which is not really separable from the first one, consists in raising the notion of coincidence to the rank of a tool essential for understanding social life. People willingly recognize that "chance plays a part" in what happens to them in life. But sociologists never stop constructing models in which chance has to be methodically reduced to a minimum. The same sociologists, when they are asked, for example, why they chose this line of work, willingly recognize the fortuitous nature of the circumstances, the encounters, the readings, and the particular opportunities that led them to choose this career. Nevertheless, they ordinarily seek to work out theories in which the choice of an occupation is severely limited and in which certain decisions are made with sufficient regularity to make the choice almost predictable; in short, the role played by chance in decision making is only anecdotal and insignificant. In other words, science's work consists in reducing chance as much as possible; if chance were to play an important role, it would be hard to see what a sociology could be based on. There are no influential random events, even though there were for me. This kind of contradiction annoys Becker. It led him to examine the role of random events and coincidences in people's lives and to reflect on the problem of their integration into a "more complete understanding" of individual and collective experience:

> As I thought about it, the chief problem seemed to be that while everyone recognizes that stories like these are "really the way things happen," there is no conceptual language for discussing this thing that everyone knows. When we talk as professional social scientists, we talk about "causes" in a way we don't recognize in daily life. That disparity would not bother a lot of sociologists, but it bothers me.[8]

Once again, it is by conceiving of things in terms of processes that we can arrive at an understanding that is flexible, open to chance, and yet includes the logics and regularities of collective life. Everett Hughes urged us to think about the dependence between events in terms of contingencies. The fact that a particular event happened creates a situation in which many things can now happen. We can call contingencies things on which the following step depends, and a process is a series of events that are all contingent on those that preceded them. Thus, as we have seen in studying the notion of a world of art, the creation of a work, no matter how open it is to the multiple possibilities among which the artist chooses, is nonetheless contingent on sequences of events, on successive choices made, in advance and simultaneously, by numerous other persons. The term "intercontingency," designating this collective complication inherent in every situation, enables us to address the problem in such a way that it becomes possible to provide ourselves with a truly sociological picture of the situations of individual choices, of the random bundles of possibilities that are on offer—and to escape the traditional dilemma, which is not sociological, of determinism and freedom.

Let us take an example. The shared love of a man and a woman offers little purchase for sociology's classical perspectives. Sociology generally proposes, basing itself on the intersection of sociological variables, a reading of the regularities in the choice of a mate. What kind of person spends time with, loves, and marries which type of person? And what are the statistical chances that such couples will remain together? Seeing love as an activity may allow us to gain a more complete understanding of the phenomenon. Naturally, it is based first of all on codified, conventional representations. Prized as a happy part of life, it appears against an imaginary background (the rather recent stabilization of the cultural choices that designate it, whatever the forms of the union advocated by successive generations may be) as a personal adventure worthy of being experienced: an encounter more or less tainted by Romanticism, but especially a freely chosen, common itinerary (contrary to the arranged marriages characteristic of other societies and other periods). Thus delimited as a category of desirable experience, it is extraordinarily subject to chance, to the contingencies I have just discussed. The encounter between a given man and a given woman who might come to love one another, ready as they both are for that possibility as a result of their own itineraries, of the stages of their lives already completed, is contingent on a series of acts in which chance plays an essential role (sociologists all probably recognize this for themselves but will rarely see it this way in their work).

But the individuals involved still have to love one another, or to use Becker's happy formula, they still have "to try to love one another." Here again it is a question of an activity for which there exists at a given time a conventional moderation, but which at each of its stages also arranges choices, commitments, multiple possibilities. Loving one another does seem to be a process, punctuated by conventionally defined stages, each stage completed presenting itself as a new situation holding new possibilities.

> At a given point in their relationship, it may happen that they envisage a way, among a whole range of other possible choices, of organizing their common activities. At the very beginning, one or the other of the two may propose a "rendezvous." Later on, one or the other may—in an indirect or direct way—suggest that they spend the night together. Still later, they might try to "live together." Finally, they may decide to "get married." They can also skip one of these stages, or not follow this progression at all. . . . But to the ex-

tent that there are names to designate these relations and the various stages they go through, and to the extent that most of the individuals in a given society are familiar with them and know what they mean in the framework of the structures of long-term relationships, the man and the woman concerned will be able to organize their activities by referring to these main lines. When one of the partners suggests one of these possibilities, the other knows, more or less, what is being proposed, without needing additional explanations, and the couple can then organize their lives from day to day in accord with the schemas that these cultural images suggest.[9]

The conventional ordering of the enterprise may, however, be subject to the play of contingencies that threaten to make it escape the "normal" development of the "lovers' career":

> Let us imagine a complication that is very common today: the woman, who is divorced, has two young children with her. In this case, the couple's freedom of action is limited, and there is no cultural model that suggests what they should do to resolve the difficulties that this entails. The models that serve to form couples and those that serve to raise children suggest incompatible solutions, and the partners are forced to impose something. They have to improvise.[10]

The Scale of Sociological Knowledge

Becker's perspective can also be defined as a sociology of passages and coincidences that seeks to discover how the lives of individuals and networks of interactions, only sometimes organized in institutions, are transformed; how individuals discover the new situations that are created at each stage of a collective action, how they give them form by explaining them through a certain rationalization of the action (normalization, convention), and how they give them meaning by developing a shared understanding of what they are experiencing.

Becker's sociology is a sociology of passages in the sense that collective life is viewed as a continual process of creation through the erosion and inevitable exhaustion of conventions, through the constant eruption of unprecedented situations or of unprecedented elements in situations, and through the rather broad indeterminacy of the choices offered each individual in new situations. Thus, it is also a sociology of the temporary. Constantly replayed with different possible choices, the situations are also constantly reinterpreted. Instead of a collective practice that essentially reinforces, reproduces, and, finally, incorporates dispositions, instead of a sociological identity that is characterized above all by its stability, the experience of the actors is grasped here in its indecision, its necessary transformation, its work of apprehending new situations.

It is, thus, a sociology of coincidences. For if individual choices are not prefigured (everyone can always act differently), if culture is not what motivates the action but rather what results from the action or, more precisely, what establishes itself between us thanks to that action, then each situation can evolve into an unforeseeable form. The subject matter of sociology is neither individuals nor collective groups but rather the trajectories of action, the processes of experiencing coincidences that define situations.

On such grounds, Becker obviously denies any possibility that sociology can predict social life. For him predictions are definitively out of reach: first, because of "the radical difficulty of taking systematically into account the millions of things that are implicated in every social situation," and second

> (supposing that this problem could ever be resolved by the use of immense data banks) because we cannot say how or why people who are in a situation to evaluate the alternatives and define a strategy make this choice and not that one; and finally because it is even less possible to establish the way in which an actor's path will intersect the other, equally indeterminate paths of all the actors with whom he will have to do.[11]

A Beckerian sociologist will then prefer to ask "how?" rather than "why?" In the field, asking "how?" always turns out to be more profitable; it enables us to learn more things, to elicit responses that are ampler and more complete, the person in question feeling called upon to tell a story, a part of his story. Asking "why?" freezes him by giving him the impression that he has to justify himself,[12] whereas asking "how?" opens the door to the understanding of concrete processes, and thus has greater heuristic value.

> Assume that whatever you want to study has, not causes, but a history, a story, a narrative, a "first this happened, then that happened, and then the other happened, and it ended up like this." On this view, we understand the occurrence of events by learning the steps in the process by which they came to happen, rather than by learning the conditions that made their existence necessary.[13]

To illustrate this, let us return for a moment to the example of two people who love each other, but now to those who have ceased to love one another:

> You want to understand why a couple separates? Don't look, as a whole generation of sociologists of the family has done, for the factors—in their environment, their history, or the present circumstances—that differentiate couples that separate from those that remain together. Instead, like Diane Vaughan,[14] look into the history of the breakup, all the stages in that process, the way in which the stages are connected with one another, the way in which each has created conditions propitious or necessary for the following one—in short, try to provide "the description in conceptual terms of the processes by which the events take place." The explanation of the breakup resides in the fact that the couple went through all these stages, not that its two members were this or that type of persons.[15]

The set of notions I have just emphasized, and first of all the notions of situation, coincidence, and process, require that attention be given to particular cases and that this attention be as sustained as possible. This might suggest that basically, the procedure presented here takes as its object the study of the singular, as its framework the monograph, and as its technique ethnographic observation. But that is not entirely true. Even if "nothing is the same as anything else,"[16] sociology has to confront the problem of generalization. But on what scale and in what ways?

Howard Becker is not going to try to impose his views in methodological quarrels or to tell sociology what should be its royal road to knowledge. These debates are frequent, arrogant, and potentially murderous. They are about asserting the superiority of one method over another, of the quantitative method over the qualitative or vice versa, about accepting or rejecting the representations that social actors have of their own experience, and about determining the foundations of an authentic sociological theory. Becker has little interest in such debates.

Becker follows his own path, far away from prescriptions and epistemological prohibitions, all of which he considers "mystical." The only question that concerns him is how and to what extent one can say something interesting about social life. And the different methods may all have a contribution to make,[17] with unequal chances of success depending on the particular object of research. Once this false debate has been set aside, the problem of generalization remains. And since we cannot ask Becker what we should do, we will limit ourselves to following him and watching what he does.

Starting from the singular seen as a dynamic, a process, or a "specific story," the objective is to formulate stories whose scope is more general—that is, "typical stories":

> But you aren't looking for particular stories, of the kind novelists or historians tell. You aren't looking for the specifics that distinguish this story from any other story. Instead, you are looking for typical stories, stories that work out pretty much the same way every time they happen. You don't just look for invariant effects of causes, but for stories whose steps have a logic, perhaps even a logic as inevitable as the logic of causes. From this point of view, events are not caused by anything other than the story that led them to be the way they are.[18]

A sampling of cases, or of stories, must thus be assembled. Like Hughes, or Lindesmith, Becker thinks the procedure of random sampling, which is perfectly adapted when it is a matter of determining the statistical distribution of a phenomenon in a population, is not suited to the search for typical stories, for regular processes. The purposive sampling that must be done has to be

wary of yielding to the a priori representation of what is important or to ready-made categories that invite us to include in the
object of study cases that are supposed to be typical but whose
reputation is not based on any discussion.[19] It is necessary, on the
contrary, to collect a sample that represents the whole spectrum
of practices and behaviors. That is why, in complete opposition to
random sampling, which is intended to equalize the chances that
any given case, even eccentric ones, will be chosen, in our procedure, which seeks to escape the pitfalls of conventional thought
and ready-made answers to already-formulated questions, it
is important to maximize the probability of the appearance of
strange cases.[20]

Always remembering that things could happen differently,
and assuming that they must have and must continue to happen differently, is a permanent exercise of the sociological spirit.
We must take for granted, as a matter of method, that human
experience is always broader than we assume a priori, and that no
regularity of behaviors can be considered proven if that regularity
is founded solely on the examination of a group of cases from the
center of the sampling distribution, while exceptions have been
ignored. The fundamental principle of sociological sampling is
thus: seek the exception; seek, as a matter of method, the cases
that don't fit.

> The simplest trick of all is just to insist that nothing that can be
> imagined is impossible, so we should look for the most unlikely
> things we can think of and incorporate their existence, or the pos-
> sibility of their existence, into our thinking.[21]

It will be possible to construct concepts by working on this
"complete spectrum of practices and behaviors." They will be
constructed, as the "Wittgenstein Trick" shows, by isolating the
characteristics on which the generalization is based. Becker gives
us an example of the use of the Wittgenstein Trick in the case
of the art collector. All kinds of people can possess works of art,
sometimes in rather large quantities, without being considered
collectors. The question is thus: "What is a collector?" This ques-

tion can be advantageously replaced by a quite different formulation: "What is collecting artworks?" As Goffman has amply demonstrated with regard to "total institutions," an "excellent, perhaps the best, way to enlarge the reach of a concept is to forget the name entirely and concentrate on the kind of collective activity that is taking place."[22] The trick is to ask: "If I take away from some event or object *X* some quality *Y*, what is left?" This trick helps us strip away what is accidentally and contingently part of an idea from what is at its core.[23]

This kind of treatment enables us to eliminate from our discussion the fact of possessing a more or less large quantity of artworks or the fact that these artworks have a greater or lesser value. What remains is that the collector's activity is oriented in a certain direction. Because he has a thorough knowledge of given periods of artistic creation and a trained aesthetic sensitivity, not to mention the cooperation of other actors in the construction of his collection, the collector makes informed choices and composes an object that can be called a "collection" in a world of art and can then be used in the whole set of activities that are usually organized around existing collections.

Overall, the procedure Becker prizes most is "analytic induction." This method, which is perfectly illustrated in *Outsiders*, was developed by Alfred Lindesmith and Edwin Sutherland, in direct descent from George Herbert Mead and Herbert Blumer, who had both underlined the importance of the negative case, of the example that contradicts your hypothesis, as crucial elements in the progress of scientific knowledge.

This procedure can be summed up as follows:

> When you do analytic induction, you develop and test your theory case by case. You formulate an explanation for the first case as soon as you have gathered data on it. You apply that theory to the second case when you get data on it. If the theory explains that case adequately, thus confirming the theory, no problem; you go on to the third case. When you hit a "negative case," one your explanatory hypothesis doesn't explain, you change the explanation of what you're trying to explain, by incorporating into it whatever new elements the

facts of this troublesome case suggest to you, or else you change the definition of what you're going to explain so as to exclude the recalcitrant case from the universe of things to be explained. Researchers usually rule out many cases this way and, once they have redefined them as not the kind of thing the theory is trying to explain, more or less ignore them.[24]

We see that Becker's method is based on a permanent dialogue between directly observed facts and "theory." However, it would be better not to use the latter term, of which Becker is wary, and which he often describes as a "necessary evil." He reminds us that, like Hughes, he is very suspicious of abstract sociological theorizations, which are no doubt necessary in the execution of sociological work but which nonetheless remain a way of perverting this work, in the sense that they constitute "a tool that threatens to escape our control and lead us into generalizing discourses that are increasingly cut off from the everyday immersion in social life that is the essence of research in sociology."[25] Becker prefers the modest enterprise that consists in presenting theoretical work as a set of "tricks," that is, as something that, far from being a generalization of the philosophical and ideological type, remains a set of procedures to be used in the field. They are in fact procedures for continually adjusting the sociologist's gaze and his theoretical ambition to the givens in the field that he defends. Analytic induction has the remarkable property of locating the priority and principal value of our work not in generalization and theorization but instead in facts. It always prefers to cut wide swaths through the ambition to generalize and resolutely chooses to reframe the very object of the study rather than to have to integrate awkward facts into it by fraud. Finally, it prefers to situate theory at a level where the role of exceptions is, as we say too lightly as we write them off, to "prove the rule." This sociology is an enterprise of dialogue between the real and theorization,[26] and Becker's penchant for the first of these two terms now calls for an even more careful discussion of the passion for facts that characterizes it.

5

What Is There to See, What Is There to Say?

Short Preamble on "Sociological Truth"

Beckerian sociology, and along with it a broad tendency in American sociology, within which it is included, are sharply distinguished from the habitual tendencies and reflexes of a certain kind of European sociology that focuses on the problem of the consciousness that actors may have of the stakes involved in their own action. From Durkheim to Bourdieu, a whole tradition of sociological research has been founded on suspicion. In reality, actors are supposed to be influenced without their knowing it, penetrated by structural logics that escape them and are usually inaccessible to them—unless they become sociologists, who, endowed by their method with exceptional lucidity, become capable of showing that, when actors think they are doing one thing, they are really doing something else. Believing that they are honoring some transcendent divinity, in fact they are venerating the process of social integration, and when they believe that they are enjoying some dish, they are really taking pleasure in showing how different they are from their neighbors at the dining table.

The Beckerian point of view is entirely different. He suggests that we think that actors know why they are there and know what they want in the situation they are participating in. And it is not for sociologists to pass judgment on what they want or on what motivates them or on what they like. We should not make the kind of judgment typical of sociology that sees them as not knowing what they are doing. In the rather strange relationship between the sociologist and those he is observing, truth is not a priori on the side of the sociologist, who alone can account for it because of his knowledge of the unconscious structures of social life and of the ultimate reasons the actors have for acting, which they camouflage behind circumstantial reasons. Truth is on the side of the actors, who with their own tools and in their own networks of social insertion constantly make choices that are, from their point of view, properly informed. These choices are the sociologist's horizon of truth, and the proper information the actors use to make them are the lived conditions of making these choices, the inventory of the mental material at the actors' disposal, and the dynamics of the coincidences that offer certain choices as possible.

Thus, there is nothing hidden. The sociologist's work does not consist in revealing things that naturally escape everyone else. Although it is indisputable that sociologists know things that the people they study do not, Becker and Hughes treat this fact on a level different from that of unconscious structures that are supposed to be the only ones that truly reveal experienced truths. It is approached as an effect of practice in the field, which ceases to make of it a virtually scornful postulate. Becker remembers Hughes saying: "There is nothing I know that at least one of the members of this group does not also know, but since I know what they all know, I know more than any one of them." In such a perspective, the sociologist's task is not to cast suspicion on common knowledge and to tell a truth inaccessible by nature to the actors but rather to glue back together the bits of knowledge that are in the possession of various individuals and, in addition, to understand the collectively established mechanisms that cause this knowledge to be distributed as it is.

Referring to the study of college students he carried out with Blanche Geer and Everett Hughes,[1] Becker arrives at the conclusion that in fact, both as a team and individually, the authors knew more than any of the participants in the campus's political life. Nevertheless,

> knowing these things didn't mean that we felt superior to the people we studied or that we thought we could find meanings in the events they participated in that were too subtle for them to understand. That would indeed be disrespectful. But it did mean we knew obvious things that the people involved would have understood quite well, had they had access to them. The reason they didn't know them was not that they were stupid or uneducated or lacking in sensibility, but that campus life was organized so as to prevent them from finding out. Saying that does not indicate disrespect for anyone's experience, but rather respect for the reality of the differential distribution of knowledge Simmel described in his essay on secrecy.[2]

But to discover these things and to rearticulate them, we have to carry out a serious investigation that leads to a thorough understanding of what people do together, namely, among other things, sharing both knowledge and ignorance. We have to complicate it this way to understand the principle according to which "what everyone knows is the object of our study."[3]

Seeing More

Freed from suspicion, sociological investigation remains confronted by a problem that is philosophically commonplace and, it seems, philosophically insoluble: that of "categories." We represent our lived reality through categories that shape our thought in advance and of which we have little or no awareness. Claiming to purely and simply rid ourselves of these would amount to supposing that our thought can be founded outside our own culture, which makes no sense. Thus, it is to our advantage to redefine the problem, to extract it from the philosophical dilemma and treat it as a practical problem of research. Since our mental tool box prefigures the answers to our questions and provides us with conventional representations of the objects we are studying, and since we are therefore tempted to think that everything can be taken for granted, it is worthwhile to set up strategies of observation that are capable of disturbing the certainties that we have acquired in advance.

The first of these strategies, which I won't linger on here because it has been discussed in the preceding chapter, consists in systematically looking for the exception. This Beckerian reflex regarding sampling is in fact capable of opening up to investigation and to sociological curiosity an angle sufficient to put in doubt the a priori conceptions that we might have concerning the way things happen in this or that domain of social life.

The second strategy has to do with techniques of observation and notation. More than anyone else, Becker insists on the aspect of sociological work, which is often considered unclear, that consists in taking notes on the basis of observation in the field. Taking notes is an entirely different thing from writing a report. Problems are constructed by the sociologist, and they are constructed precisely from facts picked out and taken down in writing. That is why the art of writing plays such a major role in Becker's thought. He insists on making his own writing clear and simple, comprehensible for everyone, especially for those about whom he is talking, and that is a political position on his part. But he has also conducted, with his students, a thorough analysis of sociological writing.[4]

A good way of constructing problems consists—and even this is obviously an ideal that is impossible to attain—in observing and noting down to the point of providing oneself with "an entire and complete description," because "careful description of details, unfiltered by our ideas and theories, produces observations that, not fitting those categories, require us to create new ideas and categories into which they can be fitted without forcing."[5] This kind of minute observation requires learning how to see and how to take sociological notes. Direct observation always has a disarming character. In general, we are overcome by the feeling that there is not much to see, and that there is nothing notable—that is, nothing interesting. We understand, or think we understand, too well and too quickly the reason why things are organized as they are, why people are there and what they are doing. We have to surmount this first impression methodologically and relentlessly continue the exercise of taking notes all the same, noting down even more, even what is not "notable." You have to learn to constitute as material for reflection things, facts, and actions that do not seem worth thinking about. You have to substitute description for interpretation, and to do that, you have to practice picking out "what happens when nothing is happening":

> The idea that we should only attend to what is interesting, to what our previous thinking tells us is important, to what our professional world tells us is important, to what the literature tells us is important, is a great pitfall. Social scientists often make great progress exactly by paying attention to what their predecessors thought was boring, trivial, commonplace.[6]

It is not surprising that while following this road, Becker was attracted by Georges Perec's work. Perec, the French novelist, was an adept of the "massively detailed description" that Becker advocated. In *Things: A Story of the Sixties*, in *A Man Asleep*, in *Life: A User's Manual*, and in *An Attempt at Exhausting a Place in Paris*, Perec practices intensive description.[7] In the latter book, which remained unfinished, he planned to describe a few places in Paris, visiting each of them once a year, never the same month, in order to obtain, after twelve years, a complete description of each site for every month of the year. It was an exercise in noting down the commonplace: buses passing, the perpetual dance of the pigeons, little street events, when there are any, but there are hardly any. Nonetheless, something is always happening. The place is crossed by people, by pedestrians, cyclists, and motorcyclists, by cars, taxis, buses. It is traversed by symbols, numbers, letters, colors. It is invested by movements, in an increasingly complex rhythm. All this is of no importance. No event suddenly occurs. It is the simple course of urban life in its public spaces, when

nothing is happening. But Perec's systematic notations render
an account of what is only very rarely mentioned in sociological
studies and is generally cut out in film scenarios: namely, what is
for most residents their actual experience of the city for a non-
negligible part of their time. These notations may be stockpiled
as a neutral expression of everything one must normally expect
when one takes one's first step in the city, things we generally
become aware of only when an uncommon event occurs, when
something goes wrong, when a cyclist has just been hit by a car
driving the wrong way. It is thus a testimony of prime importance for what might be a sociological collection of the range of
elementary facts, of shared expectations, with regard to situations
that we might be about to populate, for an instant.

> Perec's strategy thus overlaps more than a little with what at least
> some kinds of social scientists set out to achieve: the description of
> what a group of people interacting and communicating under par-
> ticular historical circumstances have produced as a body of shared
> knowledge, understanding, and practice—what is usually called
> culture.[8]

Another example of massive description Becker frequently
refers to is the work of the photographer Walker Evans and the
writer James Agee, *Let Us Now Praise Famous Men*.[9] The extremely detailed nature of the description and the complementarity of its verbal and visual aspects make this work a first-class
document. But is it really just a simple document? Becker does
not hesitate to call it a great classic of sociology.[10] For such a
work does more than just illustrate. After all, illustrating always
means illustrating *something*, and in the case of sociology, most
of the time illustration is only an anecdote with regard to theory.
Here, on the contrary, such a precise and complete description
makes it possible to understand in a striking way what is or was
the lived experience of men and women in certain historical situations. And with regard to such documents, theory is no longer
necessary. The descriptions can provide an account, in their own
way, "of what everyone in a specific historical and social context

knew and felt. What [they] drew our attention to is what seems unimportant, what doesn't deserve commentary, what (certainly) does not deserve a theoretical account."[11]

Photography and Sociology

Visual sociology remains in its infancy. Unlike anthropology, sociology has not from the outset included the image in its reflective procedure. Considered at best unnecessary and at worst illegitimate, the photographic image not only remains rare in sociologists' journals and books but has not been subjected to sustained examination regarding its heuristic value for the discipline.

In this domain as well, Becker is an exception. He learned the practice of photography, has devoted numerous studies to it,[12] and continues to look into the possibility that photography might constitute, in sociology, "a particularly suitable method of research."[13]

Becker's response to the central question regarding the conditions under which photography can be used in sociology and what services it can render to it is worked out on several levels. First of all, the photographic object—the published picture—has to be questioned, since it comes from somewhere, since it has been produced, disseminated, and looked at under certain conditions and thanks to a socially organized process. Whatever type of photography one is dealing with—amateur, commercial, art, or documentary photography, the latter being pertinent to the intellectual interest closest to that of sociology—all works resulting from these different activities can be subjected to an analysis analogous to that carried out on works of art. Taking photos is a kind of work, and naturally, it is something people do together. It implies, around the photographer, the presence of different categories of actors, support staffs, and equipment whose availability and technical expertise prove decisive. It is based on photographic conventions. But as always, in art as in life, all this work is organized into a process of playing with conventions, and at each step in this process the photographer is confronted by choices. The case of photography is no doubt particularly interesting and revealing insofar as the stages of the process are more clearly marked in a series of operations that all call for choices but that are here more isolated, more technical, and thus more visible than in work in the theater or as a painter, for example. A whole series of choices determines the final result of the work: the decision to use this or that type of lens, this or that kind of film, the choice of framing and of settings, and, later on, choices related to the sensitivity of the photographic paper, the length of time it is exposed to light in the enlarger, how long the paper is left in the developing bath, not to mention the crucial choice of which picture on the contact sheet, among all the other more or less similar pictures of the same subject that professionals usually take, is printed.

The question about the relationship between photography and sociology has meaning only when it is raised, first of all, in this way. It is only when we have understood who made it and how it was made that we can examine it with regard to what it allows sociologists and publics to see. How do we find meaning in photographs? What shared understandings can emerge from a "reading" of this type of documents? To decipher this process of reading, Becker relies on an example, that of Walker Evans's collection *American Photographs*, which is doubly interesting: first, because its author, a great documentary photographer, intended here to sketch a portrait of authentic American culture and, second, because the photos are not accompanied by captions or any of the other elements that usually serve as a guide to the interpretation of photographs.

A single photograph of this type deliberately includes a great quantity of information, and there is always so much to see that each image can "tell more than one story."[14] So, then, how can we go about discovering what is important, what we are supposed to derive from the photo? Our understanding is guided by a device, that of *montage*, which is intentionally practiced by the author and nourished by operations of comparison. For a photographer put in a situation like the one Evans found himself in, having to publish eighty-seven photos without captions—whether in a book or in an exhibit—it is difficult to choose an order, to establish the photographic environment of each picture, on which a large part of our reading depends, because the whole set of photos, placed before and after the one we are currently looking at, conditions our understanding of this one.

From the observation of two and, then, of several photos, we notice one or several common elements that we provisionally focus on for what they have to tell us. This is the same process that we use for music and poetry, as Leonard Meyer and Barbara Herrnstein Smith respectively have shown.[15]

> We of course test the hypothesis with succeeding pictures, as Meyer and Smith suggest we do in listening to each succeeding bar of music or reading each successive line of a poem. So we look at a third picture, seeing if it has the features our hypothesis about similarities suggests. When (as is usually the case) it doesn't do that exactly, but does do it partly, we revise our hypothesis, our notion of what the sequence is about, to take account of this variation. And so on, comparing each next picture, again and again, to what has come before, using our accumulated understanding of the similarities to arrive at an understanding of what the whole sequence is about.[16]

In doing so, the reader of photographs does nothing different from what a reader of statistical tables does, comparing figure by figure until he has an overall view of the meaning of the whole of the data collected, except that the reader of photographs has to simultaneously make the comparison and construct the table that organizes in large categories the data in question.[17]

When these procedures have been established, there remains the question that sociologists may consider the main one: do photographs tell the truth? To what extent can we trust them as testimonies about social life? Becker's whole argument pleads for an ambiguous answer to this kind of question. As sociologists, we have to conduct an ongoing investigation into the methods of explaining society, whether they proceed through words, numbers, or images. Photographs are not in themselves either truer or more erroneous than other means available to us for revealing social life. They constitute a procedure equal in performance to any other, provided that care is taken to analyze the actual choices and the collective conditions under which they are made, from which proceed the data that we have at our disposal. The same questions regarding the choices at work—and regarding the conventional character of all knowledge—have to be constantly raised in the social sciences. Photographs, like all the mediations that investigation leads us to use, can respond to all our questions, but they can help us only if we help ourselves by questioning our ways of questioning:

> For all of us (photographers and sociologists) the lesson is not to worry too much about the distinctions between information and expression, scholarship and art, for all photographs contain elements of both, depending on the interests of those who look at them. They are all answers to our questions, and, though they do not change, our questions do.[18]

In a more general way, Becker argues for an ongoing collaboration between sociological work and works of fiction. In particular, he expects literature to enact plausible plots that help us explore the fact that things can happen differently. In that way it can teach us to deconstruct sociology's ready-made categories, because "the social scientist's unambiguous concepts produce unambiguous results. The literary description trades clarity and unidimensionality for the ability to make multiple analyses of the multiple possibilities contained in one story."[19]

6

A Researcher Set Free

An Open-Air Sociology

Patricia Limerick once said that university professors are people no one would dance with in high school. And Harvey Molotch adds that they are also the last ones chosen for teams in gym class. Moreover, he clearly implies that sociologists are people who organize their lives in a way that allows them to know as little as possible about social life. Every moment not devoted to teaching, correcting tests and papers, or writing articles is used to attend the meetings of all sorts of councils, committees, and commissions. We can add that when sociologists can get away, they run off to a conference, where they will use all their spare time talking about the problems they encounter in their councils, committees, and commissions. "Sociologists often know no world outside their own academic and family daily round," Molotch writes. They don't wander around on trading floors, in churches where trance rituals are practiced, or in clubhouses at fashionable golf courses.[1] As Becker points out, this lack of direct experience ends up producing unnecessary difficulties: "an early version of Molotch's diagnosis defined a sociologist as someone who spends a hundred thousand dollars studying prostitution to discover what any cab driver could have told him."[2]

Becker is not indifferent to Molotch's conception of an open-air sociology in the grand style:

> [Molotch] describes his own youthful image of sociology as the result of a kind of amalgam of C. Wright Mills, Jack Kerouac, Lenny Bruce, and Henry Miller, "all heroes who knew the world through its edges—a deviant, strident, dirty-mouthed world." That means that if you want to write about society, you have to know about it firsthand, and in particular you have to know about the places respectable people have little or no experience of: "the taxi-dance hall, the housing projects, the protest marches, the youth gangs, and all the dark places most of us know only as haunting hints of the possible."[3]

Of course, not just anyone can be a Kerouac or a Wright Mills. But that shouldn't discourage anybody from "freeing himself from the tyranny of conventional forms."[4] Becker seldom uses expressions like that, which sound like programmatic declarations intended to refound the discipline—a little too solemn, a little too philosophical—and when we do find them, we have to realize that they are less important than a whole set of modest steps and acts of research that seek, without any guarantee of success, to shift the sociological point of view a bit, to see in a different way, to see a little more.

A Flexible Science

Since they cannot claim the status of "hard sciences," must the "human sciences" be considered "soft sciences"? Instead, I shall follow Becker in defining sociology as a *flexible science*, and this must be understood as meaning that it is both flexible in its procedures and attentive to the flexibility of the social itself. It is flexible because the procedure is constructed as it goes along. Empirical research not only constantly provides material for theoretical reflection but also constantly inflects it. As we have seen in briefly discussing analytical induction, the category of the facts studied is itself subject to ongoing rectifications because the point is not to construct a general theory that could in principle comprehend the totality of events but to achieve precise knowledge of one category of phenomena.

Even if, in his unstinting loyalty to fieldwork, Becker says that he pays little attention to existing theories when approaching the phenomenon he is studying, that does not mean that his observation begins with a tabula rasa. It is guided by a few "practical ideas" that Blumer called "consciousness-raising concepts." Becker sums up the three essential ideas of this kind, which synthesize aspects of his work that we have already encountered:

> Among the practical ideas that guide me when I am beginning to study something, three are particularly important.
>
> 1. The idea that the subject of sociology is: how do people do things together? I've learned to call this, with Blumer, a "collective action." In practice, this means that I'm always looking for all the people involved in the action I'm studying, including especially those who are conventionally not considered particularly important. In addition, this means that I consider everything related to what I'm studying, including artworks, as the product of what people do together. One of the great questions that research raises is: how do these people manage to coordinate their activity in such a way as to produce this or that result?
>
> 2. The idea of comparison, that is, the idea that you can learn things from a single case by examining another case that seems close to it in many respects but which is nonetheless not exactly the same. The fact of placing side by side two or more cases allows us to see how the same phenomena—the same forms of collective activity, the same processes—take a different form elsewhere, and to see what these differences depend on and what differentiations ensue in the results.
>
> 3. The idea of process, that nothing happens all at once, that everything occurs in steps, first this, then that, and that this never stops. So what we take as an end state to be explained is only a place we have chosen to stop our work, not something given in nature. The sociological analysis consists of finding, step by step, who did what, how they accomplished the coordination their activity required, and what came of their collective activity.[5]

Another reason that this sociology is flexible is that it "airs out the data cupboard." It refuses to rigidify and mythicize disciplinary boundaries or the methodological and conceptual tools that may be used in support of the current procedure. Formulas often used in the profession, such as "Is it really sociology? It isn't sociology!," seem to Becker completely inappropriate. He sets out to borrow freely from autobiography, from literary or cinematic fiction, and from the arts in general and photography in particular the elements of reflection that he finds useful. In the same way, he will seek in any discipline the information and concepts that sociology needs. For him, maintaining disciplinary boundaries is of no importance. He frequently reminds his colleagues in the sociology of art, who are often fond of boundaries and seek to discover what specific contribution sociology might have to make to thinking about art, that the best sociological ideas in the sociology of art have always come not from sociologists but from art historians, musicologists, ethnomusicologists, specialists in literature, etc.[6] He concludes, with the slightly provocative humor that sometimes makes his eyes twinkle, that he is an advocate of an "imperialistic sociology," which for him means: "If it's interesting, it's sociology."

A sociology of this kind seeks, not to produce a transcendent truth about the social, but to illustrate and comprehend constantly morphing social facts as they are being produced. The object of sociology is not the truth principle of the social or the exhaustion of the social by knowledge—goals that are unattainable because no universal principle is the source of energy and the regulator of the social and because the social is constantly reinventing itself. Its object is more modest, but we can agree with Becker that it is preferable to any other: saying something interesting about the real lives of people who exist.

A flexible science is one whose knowledge of collective phenomena requires that particular attention be given not so much to structures and systems as to the actors and to the staging of their relations, to situations, and to the necessary work they often do by inventing their common life and its forms and meanings.

The approach and method of such a science lend themselves to the daily emergence of the unpredictable: in short, a flexible science is a science of freedom.

A Sociology of Freedom

Anselm Strauss once told Becker that every author's work could be summed up in a single word, and that Becker's word was "freedom." One could hardly be more synthetic or precise in characterizing Becker's work. Nevertheless, the word "freedom" must not be understood in a philosophical sense here. It is not a matter of discoursing on the necessary conditions of the possibility of human freedom in general or of praising freedom as a value. It is a matter of focusing on particular situations, moments, and places that appear as bearers of indetermination.

Let me repeat that Becker's sociology is in no way systematic. It feels no need to generalize problems or to attribute to social structures the responsibility for everything that might happen. He is often reproached for practicing a sociology that is insufficiently historical and insufficiently general and for giving too much weight to consensus, to the detriment of conflict and in particular of what sociology often considers the conflict of all conflicts, "class struggle." To these criticisms, and particularly to the last, he replies on two levels: first, by illustrating the reality of sectors of collective activity that are not dependent on the interplay of social classes. When he began to work on the sociology of art, he faced a tradition of thought that posited that works of art were bearers of meaning, and that this meaning was related to general social structures, and especially to class struggle. In his favorite domain, music, he had to concede that, in itself, music had nothing to say, and a peculiar sleight of hand was necessary to attribute to it meanings related to social structures or classes. He responded by distancing himself from the unifying conception that claims that in the final analysis everything is related to the action of a dominant factor of the collective organization. It is not that Becker denies the existence of social classes. He simply qualifies their power and their ability to unify meanings. "OK, there are social classes, so what?" he sometimes said. They can be operative in some aspects of collective life and absolutely inoperative in others, varying in importance depending on the moment, and sometimes becoming involved, in the form of representations, in lived situations.

What is said here about social classes also holds for any principle that is supposed to be a universal generator of collective life, and this constitutes the second level of Becker's response to sociologies of conflict and class. If this unification does not take place de facto, nothing justifies a unification of knowledge: thus no general theory. For his part, Becker claims for his work the status of a point of view that does not exclude other points of view and has to be judged not by its ability to embrace all the aspects of an experience but by its ability to say interesting things about certain aspects of certain problems. Thus, *Art Worlds* does not exhaust the sociological problem of art, and it makes no attempt to do so. *Outsiders* does not cover all the questions relating to the uses of marijuana, since it limits its inquiry to those who smoke for pleasure and to the way they learn how to take pleasure in it. Becker's approach is knowingly and deliberately partial. Even if, as has been said, it seeks avenues leading to a generalization, it always begins by circumscribing fragments of experience. This should not be considered a limit or a handicap. Indeed, it is the very condition of the fertility peculiar to Becker's sociology, which consists, I think, in this: a sociology that does not take the general as its object is not forced to erase extremes, to focus on the average, to attenuate contrasts. On the contrary, we have seen how our author was always seeking the exception, and we have seen again, in the discussion of Harvey Molotch, how much sociology can learn from the exploration of the marginal, from observing the exceptional areas, from dialogue with outsiders. It should engage with people considered pariahs, those who are unconventional. Conventional life is not without interest in itself, but it has to be understood that the most interesting object of sociology is not what is shared by most people—what inquiries and opinion polls usually seek to discover. The most interesting object for sociology is what is possible. The situations, therefore, in which the contrast is accentuated, in which the possible emerges, are the most interesting. The crux of the problem is always the fact that things can happen in a different way, and sometimes do.

Clearly, sociological analysis should not be specialized to the point of making it a kind of "sociology of the exception." Becker's whole approach shows us that the exception itself is formed and reinforced, step-by-step, in its interaction with normalized and normalizing practices—conventional behaviors that we find rigidified in the form of institutions. But refusing to give power to power is still a way of contributing to a sociology of freedom, of not granting too much power to the structures and mechanisms of domination. We have seen that Becker's work found ways to avoid mythicizing and sanctifying norms and institutions by reminding us that they are first of all acts, collective actions, that they are performed by actors, and that they have reality and meaning only in interactions, in our joint construction—always chaotic and unstable—of shared meanings. The notion of freedom is exactly equivalent to that of the ability, everyone's ability, to participate in the common enterprise of defining, thanks to significant choices, the conditions under which it is possible to live together. It is exactly opposed to the notion of dispossession. Becker's sociology of freedom is not the optimistic side of a sociology that is supposed to unilaterally accentuate cooperation and consensus and deemphasize mechanisms of dispossession, considered as always present.[7] It is the precise opposite of all the sociologies of dispossession, which are always sociologies of large groups of the deprived confronted by the transcendence of the norm and of the institution, sociologies of overall structures that are supposed to be the bearers of more meaning than partial experiences, sociologies dedicated to speculating on the myth of the disappearance of actors.

For all that, and unlike so many others, Becker's sociology is far from sermonizing. It does not bow to any moralism, seeking neither the defeat nor the triumph of anyone or anything. It in no way seeks to be a theory of human freedom. It assigns no mission to sociology, not even that of weakening or ultimately destroying institutions, which, he says, can manage to do that very well by themselves. What characterizes his sociology, from start to finish, is its lightness, the curious sociology of a sly sociologist who seems always to be saying, "I look at things in a different way, just to see what happens."

Couldn't we, following Becker, restore a little lightness to the sociological project in general? After all, sociology is just one way, albeit a conventional one, of telling stories, whether they are "stories about others" or our own stories. More than a century ago, we agreed upon certain rules governing sociological narrative, the kind of information that interests us, and the procedures we found acceptable for collecting this information; we more or less agreed to focus on certain problems—thus excluding a far greater number of others, which we relegated either to other disciplines or to insignificance. We agreed on a certain linguistic decorum.

But sociology is not limited to its results. Just as the slightest work of art can be understood only by studying the interactions among all the actors closely or distantly involved in it, sociological texts or theories have to be considered the result of a conventional collective action. So we have organized our work, developed our rites, established our institutions, and set up countless committees that provide, among other things, certificates of scientific validity, social urgency and worldly elegance in the rank ordering of the problems to be dealt with, and the international circulation of reputations.

We have done this together. And, as always, we could have done it otherwise. We could have chosen other ways of dividing things up (e.g., by not isolating "sociology" and instead bringing problems together under the umbrella of a science of human beings), we could have emphasized other information and other ways of gathering and sharing it, we could have given priority to different problems, and we could also have skipped committee meetings (even more than we usually do) and gone off to wander around among the men and women on the street.

Sociology has not always existed, and it will not always exist. When it ceases to exist, that will not be because it has exhausted all the problems it is concerned with or because they have exhausted themselves; it will be simply because people will feel a need, for reasons that are still entirely unforeseeable, to agree on another way of telling each other our stories, stories that are interested in the way we do things together.

Introduction to the Appendixes

HOWARD S. BECKER

Each of the following appendixes, in one way or another, reflects on the relationship between me and Alain Pessin. It seems appropriate to add these to his interpretation and appreciation of my work.

Briefly, Pessin and I met in 1999, when he invited me, out of the blue, to come to Grenoble and take part in two large *colloques*, what we call in the United States "conferences," and receive an honorary doctorate from Pierre Mendès-France University, where he taught sociology. There was a catch: I had to deliver the talks I was going to give at the *colloques* in French. My French was rudimentary, but when he agreed to translate what I would write in English so that I could stumble through it in French, I agreed.

That epitomizes an important part of our interaction over the years that remained to us until his untimely death. He was definitely a teacher and he wanted me to learn. Like all good teachers, he was also a wonderful pupil: he wanted to learn. So, in the best way, we learned together and taught each other; there's no good word for this kind of reciprocal connection.

The best way to explain this mixture of teaching and learning that we played out is to show you some of the written results. The written results are by no means the whole story, since there was a lot of talking and a lot of informal learning too.

The most important written result is, for me, certainly the book you have in your hands, Alain's (it doesn't feel right for me to speak of him more formally) thoughts and analyses of my work, born of his desire to explain what I did to his French colleagues and students. There is no greater compliment than to have someone as smart and sensitive as he was to explain your work to others, and thereby to you yourself. I learned a lot about what I do and how I do it from his explanations.

The three pieces that follow each have a little story. The first and perhaps most important one is the dialogue we created in written form about the meaning and appropriate use of the terms "field" (*champs*) and "world" (*monde*) in sociology. I had appropriated "world" (*monde*) to connote my vision of the kind of social organization involved in the making of artworks, using it to refer to the observable fact that it took a lot of people, other than the one usually credited for the result, to make an artwork. This ran at cross-purposes to *champs*, the word Pierre Bourdieu, certainly the most well-known sociologist in France at the time, had chosen to embody his vision of what was involved in this difference about how to analyze art sociologically, and the result was that for many people, especially but not only in France, the distinction between the two terms had something of a political meaning, "political" in the professional sense. To use one or the other was in some way taking sides in a professional struggle.

For me, as it would be for almost anyone coming from the much larger world of North American sociology, this was not an important professional matter, since no one could possibly exert serious power over the scattered and various components of that world. But in France it had much more resonance, and people spent time trying to sort out the differences between the two terms and their possible meaning and consequences. Alain thought that this discussion (in which neither Bourdieu nor I had taken part) was confused and that, if I agreed to participate, we could do something to sort out the issues involved. We did that in writing, with Alain writing to me in French, and me writing to him in English. We both thought that we had perhaps provided some clarification. The piece was first published in France and, a few years later, in the United States (he translated my English and I translated his French). We might have done more collaborating but his illness and death made that impossible.

And this explains the other two items presented here. The first, appendix B, consists of brief remarks I delivered at a memorial meeting in Grenoble, where I was one of many people speaking about what Alain had done for them—I wasn't the only one to have benefited from his counsel and intellectual companionship.

Later on, a larger and more strictly professional meeting provided the occasion for many of us to consider his work in greater depth. I had read his books on the anarchist tradition and utopian thinking, admired them greatly, and thought I could best express my appreciation for what he had done for me by writing about just that. As a token of respect, I wrote it in French, which does not come naturally or easily to me—and it appears here in English (appendix C) for the first time. It describes as simply as I can some of the many important things I learned from him, things that have shaped, and continue to shape, the sociology I do.

Appendix A: A Dialogue on the Ideas of "World" and "Field"[1]

HOWARD S. BECKER AND ALAIN PESSIN

ALAIN PESSIN: Howard Becker, the idea of "world," which you have explored fully in *Art Worlds* (1982), has aroused great interest among sociologists of art, in France as elsewhere in the world. It appears in many works, but one nevertheless has the feeling that the uses it is put to are not always very clear and do not do it justice. It is often minimized, reduced in its range and significance to the single positive virtue of cooperation. It is sometimes purely and simply denied in its specificity when it is finally turned into a more optimistic variant of what Pierre Bourdieu has called "field." Thus, many authors—professionals as well as graduate students—think that the concepts of *field* and *world* simply refer to two interchangeable approaches that are equally useful in the same research project, one emphasizing conflict, the other the complementarity of actors and actions. In this view, sprinkling a little Becker on Bourdieu would produce good sociology, if only because it would make the world seem a little less desperate place. It seems to me that this would be too simple-minded, an insufficiently rigorous use of the idea of world. That's why I think it is time to clarify this idea, and to see, with you, how it differs from and is opposed to the idea of field. Let's begin with this latter idea. What does the idea of a field evoke for you?

HOWARD S. BECKER: I've just finished reading Pierre Bourdieu's autobiography, published after his death, and so I've had a chance to see how he uses the idea in practice.[2] The book starts with a description of the *champ universitaire* as it existed when he entered it in the late 1950s. He describes it as dominated by Sartre and his followers. He says that philosophy was the important discipline, that sociology and social science were not taken seriously, except to be seen as dangerous tendencies to be suppressed. Sociology, in particular, was seen by Sartre and his followers as too American, too positivist, too much opposed to the dominant myth of the solitary intellectual who achieved the great things he achieved by, as a friend of mine used to say, "thought and thought alone."

He puts this description in the language of *field*. I'll try to summarize the imagery he uses. First of all, the idea seems very metaphorical, the metaphor coming perhaps from physics. There is a defined and confined space, which is the field, in which there is a limited amount of room, so that whatever happens in this field is a zero-sum game. If I have something, you can't have it. Naturally, then, people struggle and fight over the limited space. The people who control the limited space try to keep it all for themselves and their allies and prevent newcomers from getting any of it.

Space here is a metaphor for anything that people want that is in limited supply. For Bourdieu, this is often esteem or recognition, but it can also be more material stuff like money or access to publication outlets, things like that, "real" things, you might say.

The field is organized as "forces" of various kinds, and one big force is power, which seems to involve the control of resources: in the case of the *champ universitaire*, these would be things like, as I said above, *postes* (permanent positions) in faculties and research centers, money to support research, access to publication outlets, and, in a general way, esteem, honor, recognition, and so on.

The people with power make judgments about newcomers, deciding whether they can be admitted to the circle of the powerful, perhaps in a subordinate role at first, or whether they must be rejected. He says that these determinations are made on the basis of the work people do but also on more personal criteria: their behavior, the way they dress, their accents, their political ideas, their friends, their lovers. (He doesn't quite say that the latter are illegitimate criteria, although perhaps he does somewhere, but he certainly means that you should understand him this way.) Although the idea is meant to be completely general, the examples (naturally, since it is autobiographical) come from the French university system of the 1950s.

ALAIN PESSIN: The idea of field should be generalizable to all areas of social life, including the one that interests us directly, artistic activity.

Having proposed, with the idea of world, a very different approach, what point, would you say, separates you most clearly from Bourdieu's approach?

HOWARD S. BECKER: The idea of field seems to me much more a metaphor than a simple descriptive term. Bourdieu described the social arrangements in which art is made—what he calls a field—as if it were a field of forces in physics rather than a lot of people doing something together. The principal entities in a field are forces, spaces, relations, and actors (characterized by their relative power) who develop strategies using the variable amounts of power they have available.

The people who act in a field are not flesh and blood people, with all the complexity that implies, but rather caricatures, in the style of the *Homo economicus* of the economists, endowed with the minimal capacities they have to have to behave as the theory suggests they will. Their relations seem to be exclusively relations of domination, based in competition and conflict. When I try to imagine such a field, I see a diagram: a square enclosing a space in which arrows connect units, creating invisible structures. Or, worse yet, I imagine a big plastic box with all kinds of rays shooting around inside it, like something you would see in a science fiction movie.

The repetition of the physical metaphor is very striking in *The Rules of Art*. For example, in the section at the beginning of the book entitled "The Question of Inheritance," he says,

> In thus laying out the two poles of the field of power, a true *milieu* in the Newtonian sense, where social forces, attractions or repulsions, are exercised and find their phenomenal manifestation in the form of psychological motivations such as love or ambition, Flaubert institutes the

conditions of a kind of sociological experimentation: five adolescents—including the hero, Frédéric—provisionally assembled by their situation as students, will be launched into this space like particles into a force-field, and their trajectories will be determined by the relation between the forces of the field and their own inertia. This inertia is inscribed on the one hand in the dispositions they owe to their origins and to their trajectories, and which imply a tendency to persevere in a manner of being and thus a probable trajectory, and on the other in the capital they have inherited, and which contributes to defining the possibilities and the impossibilities which the field assigns them.[3]

ALAIN PESSIN: What evokes such images is in some way the "compression" of the social. The virulence of the oppositions is inevitable because of the fundamental scarcity of the space and, as a result, the scarcity of positions anyone can occupy. The idea of world puts us in an extendable, open space, to which, moreover, it's difficult to assign limits, insofar as the spatial metaphor is relevant to it at all.

HOWARD S. BECKER: The idea of world, as I think of it, is very different. Of course, it is still a metaphor. But the metaphor of world—which does not seem to be at all true of the metaphor of field—contains people, all sorts of people, who are in the middle of doing something that requires them to pay attention to each other, to consciously take account of the existence of others and to shape what they do in the light of what others do. In such a world, people do not respond automatically to mysterious external forces surrounding them. Instead, they develop their lines of activity gradually, seeing how others respond to what they do and adjusting what they do next in a way that meshes with what others have done and will probably do next.

Above all, the metaphor is not spatial. The analysis centers on some kind of collective activity, something that people are doing together. Whoever contributes in any way to that activity and its results is part of that world. The line drawn to separate the world from whatever is not part of it is an analytic convenience, not something that exists in nature, not something that can be found by scientific investigation.

So the world is not a closed unit. Sometimes, of course, there really is a bounded area of activity, such as the university world, in which some set of organizations and people monopolizes the activity in question. Some forms of collective action have walls around them, not just the total institutions Goffman described but also all the companies where you have to have a badge to get beyond the reception area and, in the cases Bourdieu focuses on, those places where physical access isn't limited but access to positions and activities is.

In these cases, you might say, the field, limited as it is by rules and practices that keep outsiders out, makes it impossible to be part of some collective activity unless you are chosen by the people who already are part of it. You can't do sociology or intellectual work if you are denied access to the places where people are doing that sort of work together. So you can't be a sociologist unless you can have a job in a sociology department or research center and can publish your work in the recognized places where sociology is published.

To say it that way raises obvious problems. Even in such cases, the monopoly is almost never complete and certainly is never permanent. So, as Bourdieu describes the world that was the setting for the beginning of his career, doing sociology was not confined to the places he seems to care about most. It was not only at the Sorbonne or the Collège de France that sociological work got done. He never mentions, for example, Georges Friedmann, who was a friend of my mentor, Everett Hughes, and who studied factories, the industrial world.

I suppose a Bourdieusien might say that, well, of course, you could do something that would look like sociology and might even be sociology, from some point of view (maybe, as in the case of Friedmann, from the point of view of a visiting American industrial sociologist), but, let's face it, it wouldn't really be sociology because the people who own the trademark wouldn't recognize you as doing the real thing. "Congratulations, Friedmann, looks like interesting stuff; too bad no one knows or cares about you." The equivocal term here is "no one," because of course people knew about Friedmann, but the people who counted, in Bourdieu's view, didn't accept him.

At this point it is, as we like to say, an empirical question: is it true that someone can control access to everything important in that way? Can your heterodox ideas be prevented from reaching some public if the "important people" ignore them? That depends.

I think that probably it is not really very common, although it is common for people to feel that this is what's happening to them and their ideas.

At this point I think it might be useful to consider the differences between the institutionalized academic and intellectual life of the United States and France, and even to engage in some speculation about the sources of those differences. I have for years been telling people in France that to understand American sociology they must first understand that there are something like 20,000 sociologists in the United States and something like 2,000 departments of sociology (and many sociologists work in other fields—education, social work, nursing, etc.—thus making the number even larger). This is at least ten times the number of people and departments that exist in France, probably more like twenty times.

One consequence of this is that it is relatively easy to support a wide variety of sociological activities. No idea is too crazy or unacceptable to find a home somewhere. You name it, and there is, somewhere, a department or a part of a department devoted to propagating that idea or point of view. You can always find some other people who think your idea, unacceptable as it is to "the leaders of the field," whoever they are, is really good and are ready to march under your flag. If you can find two or three hundred of them (not so easy, but certainly not impossible when there are 20,000 from whom to recruit), you can organize a section of the American Sociological Association. If you can't get that number, you can start your own organization (e.g., the International Visual Sociology Association), publish your own journal, elect your own president, and give your own prizes.

It's in that sort of setting that the idea of world seems like a "natural" way to think about organized activity.

ALAIN PESSIN: One could summarize all this in one of your favorite ideas: "You could always do something else." But this idea has to have a general application; it's not only in the United States that you can do something else. Such a formula, when you apply it to any situation of social life, opens the way to a sociology of the possible; it stands in opposition to the idea of limited possibilities of action and the blocked aspect of social systems. When you aren't wanted in one place, you can always go someplace else and do what you want to do there.

HOWARD S. BECKER: Someone is monopolizing the field you want to work in? Move somewhere else and start your own field. You don't even have to compete with the other people. You can criticize them to your followers, or ignore them, but they are not powerful enough and do not have enough of a monopoly to prevent you from doing anything.

Remember that even in totalitarian regimes there were almost always dissident intellectual movements doing things forbidden by the people who dominated the legitimate field for that kind of work. When the Brazilian military juntas forbade academic sociology, people organized research institutes—with outside help, of course—and began to practice "urban anthropology," which was not forbidden. (Of course, there are extreme cases where it is impossible to escape the power of the leaders of a field, but I think that, empirically, that isn't frequent, and certainly not at all in the case of artistic activities in most contemporary societies.)

So the idea of a world of people who collaborate to produce this or that result, a world in which people can find others to collaborate with even if the more powerful people in their discipline don't approve of or recognize what they do, a world in which the power to define what is important or acceptable is not held by only one set of actors—in that sort of situation, the idea of world makes sense and is analytically useful, because it takes into account what is there to be discovered, what events there are to explain.

In contrast with the idea of field, the idea of world seems to me more empirically grounded. It talks about things that we can observe—people doing things rather than "forces," "trajectories," or "inertia," which are not observable in social life, if you understand these terms in the technical sense given to them in physics. We cannot observe these things perfectly, of course, but well enough that we can argue about them, and the procedures of empirical science can give us provisional answers of the kind science gives.

ALAIN PESSIN: A "world" is thus an ensemble of people who do something together. The action of each is not determined by something like the "global structure" of the world in question but by the specific motivations of each of the participants, any of whom might "do something different," create new responses to new situations. In these conditions, what they do together results from arrangements about which the least one can say is that they are never entirely predictable.

HOWARD S. BECKER: A "world" as I understand it—and if my language elsewhere doesn't convey this, then I've failed to be clear—consists of real people who are trying to get things done, largely by getting other people to do things that will assist them in their project. Because everyone has a project, and the outcome of negotiations between them is whatever they finally all agree to, all those involved in such an activity must take into account how others will respond to their own actions. David Mamet, the playwright, said somewhere I can't now find that, in a scene in a play, everyone in the scene has something they want. If they didn't want something they wouldn't be there, they'd be off someplace where they could pursue something they did want. The scene consists of each one trying to get what he or she wants, and the resulting collective activity is something that perhaps no one wanted but is the best everyone could get out of this situation and therefore what they all, in effect, agreed to.

This means that while people are free to try to find other possibilities, those possibilities are limited by what they can force or persuade other people to do.

This approach perhaps makes social life seem more open to continuous change and spontaneous action than it really is. Social life exhibits, after all, substantial regularity. People do not do whatever comes into their heads at any moment. On the contrary, most of the time they do things as they have done them before. In a scheme that emphasizes openness and possibility, that regularity requires explanation.

I find that explanation mainly in the idea of "convention." People often, but not always, know how things have been done in the past, how things are usually done, and they know that others know all these things too. So, if I do things as I know everyone knows they are usually done and is prepared to do them, I can feel confident that my actions will fit in with theirs, and we will be able to accomplish what we are trying to do with a minimum of difficulty and misunderstanding. This is not to say that there is not, or never has been, conflict, but rather that in most cases the conflict has been settled, one way or another, and participants in the activity have agreed to do it this way rather than one of the other ways it might have been done.

That's very abstract, so I'll give an example, taken from my favorite domain of examples, music. Musicians and composers sometimes disagree on how many notes to include between the two notes of an octave. God did not decree that there should be the twelve notes of the Western chromatic scale. Musicians in other traditions have often made other choices, and great musical traditions are founded on them. But Western musicians, over a very long time, did accept the 12-tone chromatic scale as the basis of their music. Now the instruments we play have that scale built into them, the notation we use to write music down for replaying, and everything else connected with Western music takes for granted, on the basis of shared conventional understandings, that everyone will be playing music written in that form on instruments built to play those notes. So it is always easier to play music based on that convention than music created in some other system. The cost in time and energy is much greater when you don't accept these conventions. So—here, I'm afraid, is a physical metaphor!—a kind of inertia disposes people to do things as they have been done in the past, and that accounts for a great deal of the regularity of social life.

Among the conventional understandings that produce these regularities, we will of course often find elements of coercion and force, open or disguised, that will produce inequalities and what we may feel are injustices. People often agree to things that are unfair, for lack of any better alternative.

ALAIN PESSIN: The ideas of career and process, which are essential to understanding the functioning of a world, bring us back to the fact that personal trajectories, as they confront collective situations, go through stages and that, at each step, the actors have to make choices. Thus nothing is definitively promised to anyone. One can't think successfully in terms of process when using the idea of field. Everything seems already settled in advance. The struggle is predefined as the normal framework of activity.

And the weight of the habitus makes the behavior of those affected by it essentially predictable.

HOWARD S. BECKER: Events and results are not determined that way. The history of attempts by social scientists to predict what will happen in this or that case should be sufficient to make us give up this dream. This is not just a problem of not having enough data or lacking sufficient computing power. It may be—but remember it is only a hypothesis of chaos theory, not something demonstrated—that a butterfly beating its wings in South America will produce a hurricane somewhere else in the world. But nothing like that has ever been demonstrated in social life, and I don't think it is a result we should aim for.

Imagine that we knew enough to predict some result, on the basis of habitus or something much clearer and more specific, a "variable" of the kind quantitative sociologists like to work with, for example, that Mr. Jones will have an automobile accident tomorrow. He will be drunk, his brakes will be in bad shape, and it will be raining, all things that make an accident likely. But it will also be necessary for Mr. Smith (or Mr. Somebody) to "cooperate" to produce the accident. That is, Smith will have to be in the right place for the drunken Jones to hit him, and the possibility of predicting those two events is correspondingly less likely. When you multiply probabilities, they decrease. And the accident will involve not only Jones and Smith, but also hundreds of other people. So the practical possibility of predicting any event, considering the multiple specific events that are necessary and the diminishing multiplicative probabilities, approaches zero. That includes predictions about what people will do based on habitus and similar individual qualities. Such things aren't meaningless, but they are just one among hundreds of things relevant to what people and organizations do.

You have pointed to something else important in your question. Things do not happen, events do not occur, people don't choose, all at once. Rather, these things occur in steps, in stages, and that means that every step offers the possibility of going in more than one direction—there is more than one possibility at every juncture. That means that the possible outcomes are always numerous and varied, not easily captured in a formula.

ALAIN PESSIN: It's time now to put to rest once and for all the misunderstanding attached to the idea of cooperation. We sometimes hear it said that you are the sociologist who has forgotten conflict. But trying to do something together in no way implies an absolutely peaceful conception of social relations.

HOWARD S. BECKER: I suppose that someone who wasn't trying very hard to understand this point of view could characterize it as simply focusing on cooperation. But that wouldn't be accurate. It could be true only if you understand cooperation in a very extended way, as encompassing anything that people do together in which they take into account and respond to what the others involved are doing. Collective action—two or more (usually a lot more) people doing something together—is not the same as cooperating in the more conventional, minimal understanding of that word, which has overtones of peacefulness, getting along with one another, and good will. On the contrary, the people engaged in collective action might be fighting or plotting against one another or doing any of the other things that figure so prominently in Bourdieu's descriptions of social fields.

But they might also be working together to do something (rehearsing for a concert they are going to give that night), or they might be linked indirectly, one doing something necessary for what the other does, even though they might not know each other (as the instrument-repair man fixes the broken saxophone necessary for the musician's evening performance). They might have joined forces for this one occasion, as composers who otherwise compete with each other for scarce commissions and posts will cooperate to put on a concert of contemporary music.[4] Or they might routinely work together on the particular thing that brings them together, as the players in an orchestra with a long season do.

The nature of these relations between people is not given a priori, not something you can establish by definition. It's something you discover by observing them in action, seeing what they do. If they are in conflict, you'll see that. If they are working together on a project, you'll see that. And if they do both—fight *and* work together on a project, you will see that too.

ALAIN PESSIN: So one can thus easily integrate conflict into the idea of a world, as long as you integrate it as a situation and not as an a priori overdetermination. From this perspective, situations are absolutely not reducible to some dynamic that overpowers them. The idea of field is characterized, on the other hand, not only by the omnipresence of conflict, but by the existence of the conflict of conflicts, the conflict of social classes, which overdetermines all other social relations. Conflict is, in this conception, a generating principle of social life. It seems that you don't share this point of view, beginning with the very idea of a generating principle of social life.

HOWARD S. BECKER: That's right. I don't think there is any single generating principle. It is more likely that many principles work together in one way or another to produce the messiness of ordinary life. But it's not just a matter of my taste. It is also, I'm sure, true that this way of looking at things is a more fruitful guide to research because it is more open to possibilities you hadn't thought of, which careful attention to the details of social life can suggest to you. It's better not to decide before you begin what the "important things" are.

ALAIN PESSIN: Readers of these two points of view are sometimes tempted to say that it is a photographic problem. Bourdieu uses a wide-angle lens while Becker focuses on micro-relations; one has an overarching global view; the other does case studies. And then people go on to say that, of course, case studies are inevitably partial, that they cannot get at what is really determining in social life. The answers you have already given show that it is the overarching view that is reductive, because it systematically ignores certain aspects and certain actors who are nevertheless essential and just as determining for the results of certain social arrangements.

HOWARD S. BECKER: The language of a "world" points us toward an inclusive notion of which actors belong in an analysis of art works, makes us recognize that everyone who contributes anything to what the work eventually is participates in some way in its making. That's tautological: everyone who participates in making a work participates in making it. The advantage of that tautology is that it shows us how to incorporate into our conception of art-making the people who are conventionally left out of such an analysis: the technicians, the money people, all the people I have called "support personnel." Their participation in making the work shows itself through a little thought experiment. Remove any of them from the action (in your mind—no one would let you do it in real life) and see what happens. If the caterers don't provide the meals for the people in the movie crew—well, they have to eat, don't they? If they can't eat right there, on the set or the location, they'll go someplace else and take longer, and the production's costs will go up. That means that more money must be raised or that something else won't be paid for—either one having serious consequences for the final form of the film.

The basic question of an analysis centered on the idea of world is this: Who is doing what with whom that affects the resulting work of art? The basic question of an analysis centered on the idea of field seems to me to be: Who dominates whom, using what strategies and resources, with what results? Such questions can be and often are (repeatedly in *Art Worlds*) raised in an analysis based on the idea of world, as a subset of the larger set of questions that might be asked. But that much larger set of questions cannot easily be raised by an analysis centered on Bourdieu's notion of field. Most of them, it seems to me, are set aside a priori as trivial in comparison with the "big questions" of dominance and forces.

If this is all true, then the conventional notion that you can mix Bourdieu and Becker in whatever proportions you like—according to your taste for or tolerance of conflict, let's say—is not accurate. In fact, they ask different kinds of questions and look for different kinds of answers and are not reducible one to the other.

ALAIN PESSIN: They start out with two different intentions, which is clear from the fact that the one must extract itself from common knowledge and oppose itself to common sense to construct, in theory, the truth about the social, while yours must immerse itself in lived practices, observing and taking seriously the procedures by which social actors construct what you call "shared understandings," which are the only truths that the social world can produce, those which create symbolic links between real people.

HOWARD S. BECKER: This is an important difference. Many social theories start with the premise that reality is hidden from ordinary mortals and that it takes a special competence, perhaps even a magical gift, to be able to see through these obstacles and discover The Truth. I have never believed that. To quote my mentor Hughes again, he often said that sociologists did not know anything that nobody else knew. Whatever sociologists knew about social life, they had learned from someone who was part of and fully engaged in that area of life. But since, as Simmel had made clear in his essay on secrecy,[5] knowledge is not equally distributed, everyone doesn't know everything—not because people are blinded to reality by illusions, but because things have been kept from them by institutional arrangements (which may or may not have been put in place to achieve that end). Sociologists find out what this one knows and what that one knows so that, in the end, they can assemble the partial knowledge of participants into a more comprehensive understanding. The idea of "false consciousness" is a classic example of the theory of social knowledge opposed to my own practice.

ALAIN PESSIN: A sociology of situations as opposed to a sociology of structures, process versus habitus, career versus disposition, openness versus closure, choice versus determination—the exercise of analysis we have gone through, it seems to me, shows very clearly that the idea of a world is in no way a "soft version" of the theory of fields. One could, moreover, add that it proceeds from observation, and is very suspicious of theory. These are not two differently nuanced versions of an approach that refer essentially to the same thing. They are two ways of thinking that are opposed in their intentions and, necessarily, in their results: the philosophico-sociological approach that searches for the essence of the social, which leads to the theory of fields, and the sociologico-ethnographic approach that tries to make explicit the circumstances in which social situations create links between actors, which is the idea of a world.

HOWARD S. BECKER: You have captured here the essential differences between the approaches: the one open to multiple possibilities, discovered in the course of immersion in social life; the other focused on demonstrating, on the basis of a priori considerations, the truth of an already established abstract philosophical position. I have nothing to add.

Appendix B: A Tribute to Alain Pessin[1]

HOWARD S. BECKER

It is conventional to say of someone who has left us that he will be missed. And surely Alain Pessin will be missed. I think it is necessary, in the case of someone who left us prematurely, long before any of us were ready for that to happen, to be more specific, to say just how he will be missed.

I speak for myself first, because this is the case I know best and am surest of. We met when he decided to promote me for a Docteur Honoris Causa degree at his university. This was unexpected, because we had not even met. With this honor came a lot of work, which I willingly accepted: to present two papers at colloquiums on successive weekends, and, from my point of view, even more exciting, it meant presenting a short piano recital (accompanied by Benoît Cancoin on bass), which stimulated a renewed interest in playing. This series of events changed my life in many ways: new friends, new activities, new collaborations.

Perhaps most important, Alain helped me find new dimensions to my thinking and encouraged me in many ways to go beyond what I had done in the past. He saw possibilities where I saw dead ends, helped me turn problems into opportunities. At my age, it is all too easy to think of your work as done, no more to do. But he didn't allow that and, in his calm, deceptively mild, and easygoing way, made me feel that I had a mountain of work before me to do, if only because he wanted to see what that work would look like when it was done. Our one collaboration—the interview he conducted with me on the relationship of the ideas of "field" and "world," published in this issue of the *Revue*—was just such an instance. His probing questions and incisive summaries pushed me to understand my own ideas far better than I ever had before. His modesty hides the brilliance of his contribution to this dialogue. And, of course, I was touched, but also instructed, by his reading of my own work in *Un sociologue en liberté*.

He did much more, helping to persuade me and Dianne that we really could learn another language, encouraging me to deliver talks to large audiences *en français* and to engage in quiet informal conversations. When someone treats you as though you can do something, you find that perhaps you can do what you thought was not possible.

I did not see much of Alain as a teacher, beyond what he taught me. But it was clear from the people I met in Grenoble and elsewhere that he had the same effect on them that he had on me, showing them how to make the most that could be made out of their own data, their own ideas, their own abilities. Quietly but surely, he helped them as he helped me to achieve what they might not have imagined possible. He leaves a legacy of students and colleagues who are better sociologists and better people because of his interventions. They will testify to his influence and kindness for themselves.

Not the least part of his influence is the example of his own work. There is not as much of this as we could wish for. He had many ideas and approaches he never had time to turn into finished works. But we have the books on anarchism and the book on the idea of *le peuple* and the many papers he wrote on those and related subjects. I particularly loved his essay "Le monde du velo," which he wrote for the *Mélanges* he edited in my honor with Alain Blanc.

Related to all that is the immense service he rendered to the field of the sociology of art. He organized OPUS, the network of sociologists interested in this field in France, and saw to the organization of the many colloquiums and meetings OPUS held and, knowing that the products of such meetings are so often ephemeral, saw to the publication of the many volumes of *Actes* of these meetings. This was a tremendous stimulus not only to produce work but also to the development of lasting ties among the workers in this field. He did not do all this alone, of course. But I think many will agree that without Alain Pessin's energy and leadership it would not have happened.

And, finally, we will all—all of us who knew him and whose lives were touched by him—miss the person, the warm, lively, humorous, understanding, and, finally, lovable person who was Alain Pessin. Adieu, Alain.

Howard Becker
San Francisco
January 2006

Appendix C: Four Things I Learned from Alain Pessin

HOWARD S. BECKER

Alain Pessin taught me a lot when he was alive. And he continued to teach me sociology—among other things, the sociology of political movements—during the years that followed his untimely death. To prepare this paper, I reread two of his books that treated movements seeking to increase liberty, the kind that always interested him: *La rêverie anarchiste* (1982) and *L'imaginaire utopique aujourd'hui* (1992). The rereading was a revelation. This time I was finally ready to learn. I learned, from these books, important things about a field I had never worked in and in which I was completely unschooled: the history of and thinking behind important libertarian movements, fields he was expert in.

My difficulties in this area of thought came from my insistence on seeing concrete events and actions in the social situations they occurred in, even though most of the experts on this subject habitually treated these things at the level of ideas, that is, theoretically. I am always skeptical about sociological ideas that are anchored neither in real things nor in specific acts of specific people—in short, ideas divorced from the flesh-and-blood people who had them. I had never read analyses of ideas in this domain that were based on a serious analysis of the social organization of the people who thought and reasoned that way. (Surely, such analyses must exist somewhere, but I didn't know them.) So, when Alain connected political and social ideas with the actual activities of participants in these movements, that solved my problem by making a link between a quasi-philosophical analysis and the collective activities that made up the movement. This coupling has many consequences, including the four things I learned from Alain that my title refers to.

Utopias as the Activities of a Collective

Pessin taught me, first of all, that describing an ideology like anarchism or utopianism sociologically leads to a new idea of the nature of political thought. Instead of seeing it as a system of ideas, with a definite meaning independent of the situation it's used in, you see it at as the activity of a group whose members use it, as a whole or in smaller pieces, when they construct a line of action collectively. Pessin's description of the development of political actions in an alternative political world is thus completely sociological.[1] He doesn't give in to the temptation to renounce sociology in order to create a weak imitation of a treatise in political philosophy. He approaches libertarian movements as things people did together rather than as abstract ideas.

For me, it was a second big surprise to discover that Pessin's description of this phenomenon is, point for point, almost identical to the description of musical cooperation Faulkner and I later gave (in *"Do You Know . . . ?"*), even if we didn't make this connection consciously or explicitly. We describe there how musicians, when they play together without rehearsing and without any written music, don't rely on a stock of memorized "standards." Instead, they use a variety of skills that give them the resources from which they create, then and there, a program (they say a "set list"). Sometimes they base their performance on the memory of a recording they heard somewhere. Or, perhaps, not knowing the song in question at all, they base their performance on what one player, who does know the song, plays—because the formulas out of which these songs are constructed are so familiar. A group can play a song as long as one of them knows it, because the others can pick up and construct what they need from what he does. Using these tricks, they can perform an evening of music, piece by piece. It isn't a simple reproduction of what "everyone knows" but a true collectively improvised construction.

Faulkner and I thought this description would work for any social situation. But that was just a stray thought, a possibility. Pessin showed me, through his analyses of libertarian thought and movements, that these phenomena embodied more or less the same process, in which the participants feel their way together, like the musicians, looking for the joint actions that will produce a result more or less acceptable to all the participants. His analysis does not emphasize the role of political philosophies in the development of the activities of participants in libertarian movements. In fact, he reverses the conventional causal order, putting the ideas in their organizational contexts, and thus seeing them as effects rather than causes. Here's a quotation that's representative of this facet of his thought:

> It's the nature of such a culture to continually be under construction. We're witnessing a flexible society, in which, in principle, no one has any control over the others. This open society constructs its culture to order, as an ephemeral mediation, whose forms are from the beginning presented as ready to dissolve themselves in order to enable new forms of collective experimentation. An exceptional society, then, first because it really is a society, creating links between individual actors, and whose exceptional character resides in condemning the conventional forms of social life and in refusing conventional means to ensure its own long-term stability.[2]

I learned from this how to make a concrete analysis of a group that used its philosophical and political ideas to construct itself as a collection of joint actions. In fact, you can see a philosophical system as neither more nor less than the work of some group of people. The other points I learned from Alain flow from this very general point.

Libertarian Movements as "Art Worlds"

The second fruit of my apprenticeship with Alain Pessin is double. He taught me that the idea of "world," as a technical term in sociology, had possibilities I had never suspected (I introduced it as a specialized term whose uses for understanding art I explored in *Art Worlds*). For me, it was an idea you could use to understand a work of art. That was more or less it. In its simplest form, the term insisted on the fact that a work of art is made by everyone who participates in any way in its fabrication: in the case of music, for example, that includes the composer who wrote the music and the players who played it—but also the people who made the instruments the players played, the copyists who copied the parts from which the musicians played, the ticket sellers who brought in the money to pay the players, and, very important, the audience. Each participant did something without which the work would be different. And—the other important idea in this conception— the participants coordinated their activities by referring to understandings (conventions) they shared about how to negotiate each step in the process. These shared conventions furnished the models on which one could make a great variety of varied works without any difficulty. (See the discussion between me and Pessin on the ideas of "world" and "field" in appendix A.)

Pessin's great inspiration was to appropriate the idea of "world" for a quite different arena of human activity, politics. (He makes the connection explicitly on pp. 46–48.) His analysis of utopias showed me how you could look at something as big, as fluid, and as indistinct as a political philosophy just as you would look at something as solid and specific as, for example, Broadway musical comedies in the 1930s or Florentine painting in the fifteenth century.

I had never thought of this kind of activity—modes of thought or ways of doing political philosophy or overtly political activities—as a professional activity like music, which seemed to me more "solid," but that was my weakness. As Alain showed me, if you saw these things as activities, as he did, they made more sense.

Look, for example, at utopian thought and movements as worlds similar to art worlds. Following the research program that concept implied, he immediately made a list of the participants in the activity of such a world. Without any serious reflection, I would have said the only important people were the thinkers and writers. But Alain's work showed me the error of that simplification.

He found a fruitful metaphor in the theater, describing the production of a utopian world as if it were a theatrical production, and envisaged the history of utopian movements in those terms, describing them as "theatricalizations of the political problem" (56). And, while he describes all the participants as "actors" in this theater, he's careful to note that he doesn't use the word in its current generalized sociological sense but strictly to refer to an actor in a theater.

He begins by observing that a utopia is, like a work of art, someone's work. But whose?

He of course lists among the workers who do the work of making a utopia such authors of celebrated literary utopias as Thomas More, Charles Fourier, Pierre-Joseph Proudhon, and Robert Owen, but also the lesser-known writers who furnished the founding ideas for contemporary alternative communities. (Pessin himself had done fieldwork in such a community, the Croix-Rousse de Lyon.) But that is only what is most evident: they formulated the original idea and the plans for its realization.

When they wrote their texts, these authors used the classic models of the genre. They began with a voyage in time or space to a virgin destination, where you could establish the conditions for a completely new world. Of course, they wrote at length about the philosophy of and justifications for their project, but their texts were always also filled with precise specifications of the towns and of the behavior they expected of their inhabitants.

After the writers, we find the architects and the urbanists, who transform the big ideas and sentiments of the writers into specific plans and techniques, for the streets and buildings and for everything a city requires. Pessin notes, in passing, that these people are the ones who make the durable structures that are, in the end, the most prisonlike aspect of all utopias.

Then come the poets and the artists, who criticize, perhaps ironically, who discover the problems and dissonances between the foundational ideas and the reality, and who plant the germs of disorder, the conflicts between the authoritarian dreams, in the name of equality, of the founders and the freedom of choice the inhabitants seek.

Finally, there are those who Pessin calls "the humble," the practitioners of the utopia, who are without power but who are also those who "take charge of the utopian hope," the marginalized masses.

But that isn't the end of it, because in the next chapter he adds another player, perhaps the most important actor of all: the accomplice or "walk-on," before whom the drama unfolds, that is, members of the audience. This audience will observe the dramatic action and then decide if they are interested or not. The audience can be just one person, such as an enlightened industrialist in the case of Fourier. More usually, it is the crowd of the humble who have to be convinced to support great projects of social change.

What Is the Imaginary?

When he taught me how a utopia resembles a theater, that is, how you can see it as a work of art made by the participants in a shared world, on the model of an art world, Pessin taught me at the same time a third thing, the answer to my persistent question "What is the 'imaginary'?" The word arrived in American intellectual circles from France as part of the "cultural studies" movement, often inserted in the original French as the *imaginaire*, and its meaning was never very clear, at least to me. It looked like an appropriation of what is sometimes called a *faux ami*, a "false friend," a French word that looks a lot like an English word but whose many nuances don't survive the transfer to English, where it has no self-explanatory meaning.

Alain taught me to understand this word not only when he described the partners in the construction of the "imaginary" (I'll use the English version from now on) but also, the point I want to emphasize now, by using the word "reverie" as a synonym for "imaginary." "Reverie" insists, as the word "imaginary" does less clearly, on the mental aspect of this construction.

Pessin almost always used the two words interchangeably. He insisted that neither one alluded to the social movements that might (or, equally, might not) be associated with the actions of a collectivity. The imaginary, for him, was the equivalent of a work of art in the conventional analysis of an art world. Instead of a painting or a sculpture, which you could see as an integral whole, you have something more amorphous, more difficult to define, but nevertheless just as much something constructed by a world of cooperation, a world of collective action.

And in libertarian movements, this construction performs the role played by the understandings shared by the cooperating members of an art world.

These words speak of something else, of a mentality shared by many people, thus furnishing a point of support or, better, a point of departure or, better yet, the birthplace of collective actions. This mental construction, moreover, doesn't consist of theoretical or political ideas. Not at all. On the contrary, the imaginary consists of images (probably most often visual) of things, of a great variety of men and women, of events. This collection of images, assembled in a coherent whole, is the domain of the imagination, of the imaginary. It isn't necessarily concrete; it doesn't demand that you act.

In his book on anarchism, the other movement he studied and wrote about, he said:

> We have preferred throughout our study to speak of the "libertarian reverie" rather than the "anarchist movement," because in this epoch

the latter scarcely exists as a component of society. We thus refer to a diffuse reverie fed from multiple sources, drawing in particular on romantic intuitions, which appeared everywhere in Europe and, as a result, among the only ones who became, in the true sense of the word, "anarchists." It was a movement of the soul, which sprang from an initial refusal, from a proud break, from which it searched passionately for images both just and righteous as well, often as those issuing from a generous humanitarian project. (213–14)

Then he explains, discussing the great changes that had affected this mental construction (in this case, the anarchist reverie), the changes in the mode of thought and doctrine in a political movement:

By the end of the century, if the dream was not exhausted, a cycle of the libertarian reverie had finished. We would thus prefer to date the birth of anarchism to the years 1880–90, those which exhibited . . . the exacerbation of anarchist violence, day after day, to symbolize the disenchantments and new hopes, in short, a death and a renewal. From which there developed an anarchism in the proper sense of the term, as a social movement, in which the libertarian reverie becomes a little rigid, in order to embody itself in thought and doctrine. (214)

In short, he makes a simple, brief, and clear distinction between a world of the mind (reverie or images) and a world made up of interacting people, a world of political action. So far, so good. But my central difficulty remains: isn't it, thus, this so ungraspable imaginary, simply, after all, a system of ideas?

No. The imaginary results from multiple acts of the many people who create it. Thus, it's not a system of abstract ideas, divorced from concrete actions of concrete people, but a more or less organized collection of ideas and images some people have made, remade, and continually reformulated as they used it. It encompasses and consists of a vision of the world, expressed mainly in images.

The images are, simultaneously, people's product and their most important resource, because the imaginary (or reverie) serves as a vast armory for those who want to organize a movement. Since these images last for centuries and are well known, they can be drawn on to mobilize people for a movement or a program. In fact, the use of this stock of images is almost obligatory, because everyone recognizes them as the seal of authenticity of a movement that intends to be recognized as a serious revolution. Of course, the content of this armory is always changing—Pessin himself describes the new forms they took in the libertarian community of the Croix-Rousse in Lyon—but the older forms remain alive and available.

Political movements use the imaginary as a resource flexibly. It isn't a book of recipes you can apply mechanically; it's more adaptable than that:

> A utopia imposes itself, at this level, as a style, a certain way of confronting dilemmas, a social organization and its dynamic. To understand it, you have to climb again this general structure, this utopian matrix, which is a cultural and conventional construction, which has maintained its originality and its stability through successive versions of its utopian dream. You have to return to the origin, to the process of creating this framework of a utopian imaginary. (213–14)

The Fourth Thing

Finally, what I learned from Alain had a methodological importance far beyond the specifics of libertarian movements, of anarchism and utopias. He taught me the lesson sociologists have to learn over and over again in a life of research: what you find in one area of social life can perhaps make other areas more understandable as well, even (perhaps especially) those which seem most different.

In this case, the lesson is simple but important. Every apparatus you can use to understand a world of art is useful for understanding any other form of collective action, even if that form is conventionally thought of theoretically as a world of thought rather than a system of activity. We don't ordinarily talk about ideas as a form of action, only as thoughts, without any reference to actions. That typically means looking at them as things that, belonging to a logically coherent complex of ideas, have to be understood as part of a system of logic divorced from prosaic activity and from the organizational constraints of the everyday world.

But ideas exist only when someone thinks them, when someone invents them, remembers them, or uses them in an argument. That happens in an inevitably social setting, made up of links between social actors with all the baggage of obligations and forms of cooperation and dependence that entails. Actors need a stage and a playwright and a costume maker and a director and all the others who contribute to their work. In the same way, a political thinker or theoretician needs the whole assortment described as necessary by Alain to create, for example, a utopia.

But Alain's model added some important ideas to the concept of "world," as I had described it. He put flesh on the bones of this idea when he amplified the imaginary as a receptacle of different contents according to the specific situation, thus transforming it into a marvelous resource for sociologists:

> But still, this structure [the imaginary] is, if not empty, at least hollowed out. It can be filled with the most varied, even contradictory, things, all nevertheless bearing on the same problems, concerning the possibility of inaugurating the great new society and the distribution of roles and social functions that will allow it to appear, the new relations between the individual and the collective, the stability and the dynamics of social ensembles, all this in the world made possible by the imaginary. A utopia is thus an original expression of collective hope, something people make together, even when it is elaborated by the greatest exiles, because the need for a utopia always arises in the mental framework prepared for it. This shared approach is understandable only if you look at it as the sum of its situated expressions, if you consider it collectively, as what is permanently at stake for some social ensemble, something conventionally involving a small number of mental techniques. (214)

This explanation makes the imaginary something that has enough content to avoid being empty of meaning and, at the same time, not so much content that it prevents the researcher from being open to unexpected data. What more can you ask of a concept?

Alain always said, too, that the time had come to go beyond a static conception of imaginaries to a more open analysis of the

> process of sharing imagery, and its collective dynamic, which should nourish new fields of research, after its static distribution has been studied deeply. Globally, the problem might be formulated this way: how, with what theoretical and dialectical tools, can we reconcile a conception of the image as grasped, at first, by individual participants and a conception of the image as a form of collective participation in what unites us? (216)

That's the job Alain has left to us.

Notes

FOREWORD

1. Blanc and Pessin, *L'art du terrain*, 257.
2. Gopnik, "The Outside Game," 29.

PROLOGUE

1. Becker, *Propos sur l'art*, 141.
2. *À Grenoble* (2003), a CD included with Becker, *Paroles et musique.*
3. "But most of what musicians like me played was 'commercial' music, meant for dancing (at a party or in a club or ballroom) or as background noise in a bar or club. We played most of the jazz we played by sneaking it into the performance of other kinds of music we had been hired to play.

"In short, our repertoire and style of playing were completely dictated by the circumstances of the places we played in. We knew what we wanted to do, which was to play like our heroes—in my day, the big bands of Basie, Herman, and others, the small bands of Gillespie, Parker, Stan Getz, etc. But we seldom could do that. Most of the time we played what the 'place'—the combination of physical space and social and financial arrangements—made possible" (Becker, "Les lieux du jazz," in *Paroles et musique*, 23).
4. Remarks reported in Diani, "Howard Becker, un classique de la sociologie américaine," 39.

CHAPTER 1

1. In the postface to the French edition of *Outsiders* published in 1985, Becker sums up the innovative aspect of his work this way: "This change in the conceptualization of the phenomena of deviancy finally led to what was once described as a 'scientific revolution,' to use Thomas Kuhn's expression. Researchers more and more often studied the police and the courts, or the activities of psychiatrists and of the personnel in the mental health sector, rather than the personality or social situation of deviants; a great many investigations testify to the value of this perspective. In fact, this approach did not constitute a revolution, but simply the application to this particular subject of the 'Chicago School's' theory of social organization as it had been initially developed by the works of Robert E. Park, Everett C. Hughes, and Herbert Blumer" (*Outsiders: Etudes de sociologie de la déviance*, 240). In *Doing Things Together*, Becker maintains that the so-called "revolution of the theory of labeling" was in reality a counterrevolution, a return to basic sociological ideas that had been lost—in any case, concerning deviancy—in the ordinary practice of the discipline. The principal "basic idea" being, faithful to W. Thomas's elementary program, to resort to the "definition of the situation," that is, to understand the perspective in which actors see the situation in which they find themselves, which implies both not treating them as a priori afflicted by mental troubles and, on the other hand, seeing the same thing that they do, namely, among other things, the active role of the forces of repression in the construction of the collective phenomenon of deviancy. See Becker, *Doing Things Together*, 76–77.

2. Thomas and Znaniecki, *Le paysan polonais en Europe et en Amérique*.

3. Chapoulie, *La tradition sociologique de Chicago*, 267. For a precise analysis of the notion of deviancy, and also of the whole intellectual landscape of Chicago School sociology, see this remarkably well-informed work by Jean-Michel Chapoulie.

4. Ibid., 288.

5. Becker, *Outsiders*, 26–27.

6. Becker, *Tricks of the Trade*, 12.

7. Becker, *Outsiders*, 19–39.

8. Ibid.

9. Ibid., 10.

10. However, Becker always insists on emphasizing the extent to which such ideas were in the air at the time. "I was not the only one who

was interested in saying things about deviancy. Kai Erikson (1962) had said the same thing. John Kitsuse (1962) said the same things. Lemert had said it years earlier. There were many people whose ideas were in the air. It is likely that what I did consisted in formulating something simple and clear about this question" (Becker, *Doing Things Together*, 33).

11. Ibid., 46.

12. Ibid., 43.

13. Ibid., 47.

14. Cited in ibid., 126.

15. Ibid., 48.

16. Ibid., 50.

17. Becker, *Tricks of the Trade*, 87.

18. Becker, *Outsiders*, 30–31.

19. Ibid., 38.

20. There is no need to emphasize at length that for me, as for Becker, the term "deviant" is applied to this or that practice without the slightest value judgment and arises solely from the simple observation that at a given time behaviors that are deviant may be less or no longer deviant at other times. And their definition as deviant has nothing to do with the sociologist's evaluation, but only with the play of interactions that the sociology in question here takes as its task to describe.

21. Ibid., 42.

22. Ibid., 52.

CHAPTER 2

1. Becker, *Propos sur l'art*, 8.

2. "In recent years a number of my students have studied some more or less lowly occupations: apartment-house janitors, junk men, boxers, jazz musicians, osteopaths, pharmacists, etc. . . . At first, I thought of these studies as merely interesting and informative for what they would tell about people who do these humbler jobs, i.e., as American ethnology. I have now come to the belief that although the problems of people in these lines of work are as interesting and important as any other, their deeper value lies in the insights they yield about work behavior in any and all occupations. It is not that it puts one into the position to debunk the others but simply that processes which are hidden in other occupations come more readily to view in these lowly ones" (Hughes, *Le regard sociologique*, 80–81).

3. Becker, *Propos sur l'art*, 10.

4. It was in order to be able to read Raymonde Moulin's book *Le marché de la peinture en France* that Becker learned French.

5. Becker, *Tricks of the Trade*, 85–86.

6. Becker, *Propos sur l'art*, 12.

7. Becker, *Art Worlds*, 29.

8. Ibid., 56.

9. Ibid., 34.

10. Ibid., 29–30.

11. Ibid., 14–15.

12. For example, writers often talk about the regular work that they find necessary, the number of pages per day that guarantees that they will achieve their optimal literary performance. Becker cites the case of Trollope, who thought that three hours of writing a day was a necessary and sufficient amount of work (ibid., 1).

13. Ibid., 18.

14. "Maybe the years I spent playing the piano in taverns in Chicago and elsewhere led me to believe that people who did that mundane work were as important to an understanding of art as the better-known players who produced the recognized classics of jazz. Growing up in Chicago—where Louis Sullivan's democratic philosophy was embodied in the skyscrapers of the downtown I loved to prowl around and Moholy-Nagy's Institute of Design gave a Midwestern home to the refugee Bauhaus' concern for the craft in art—may have led me to think that the craftsmen who help make art works are as important as the people who conceive them. My rebellious temperament may be the cause of a congenital antielitism" (ibid., ix).

15. Ibid., 214.

16. Ibid., 1.

17. "I learned how every participant in the making of such complex collaborative work as film thought that the resulting movie was really 'their' work, with all the others mere support personnel: film editors 'knew' that no film would be effective without their crucial skills, composers thought of films as visual accompaniment for their scores, and the writers (supported by such distinguished critics as Pauline Kael) similarly knew that cinema was really a literary art, with added visual effects" (Becker, *Propos sur l'art*, 14).

18. Ibid., 226.

19. Ibid., 34.

20. Ibid., 35.

21. Ibid., 77.

22. Ibid., 110.

23. Pierre-Michel Menger, preface to Becker, *Les mondes de l'art*, 9.

24. Becker, *Propos sur l'art*, 101–2.

25. Becker, *Art Worlds*, 163.

26. Ibid., 134.

27. Ibid., 162.

28. See especially Becker's contribution to the debate on the "sociology of artworks" begun at the Marseille congress in 1985 and continued at the "Rencontres de sociologie de l'art" meeting in Grenoble in 1999. See R. Moulin, epilogue to Majastre and Pessin, *Vers une sociologie des œuvres*, 2:468–69.

29. Becker, *Art Worlds*, 353.

30. Ibid., 226–27.

31. Ibid., 211–12.

32. See ibid., chap. 8.

33. Becker, *Paroles et musique*, 27.

34. Becker, *Propos sur l'art*, 143.

CHAPTER 3

1. Becker, *Art Worlds*, 364.

2. Becker, *Propos sur l'art*, 12.

3. Ibid.

4. Ibid., 26–27.

5. Ibid., 31.

6. Ibid.

7. Cf. ibid., 29.

8. In an article entitled "The Power of Inertia," Becker examines inertia's essentially economic conditions, from material points of view and from that of personal exploratory investment. But the observation of the frequency of inertia does not in any way lead him to maintain that the forms reproduced exercise something like an authority that is imposed on us from outside. No one, he asserts again, is obliged to do things in a conventional way. But leaving convention behind requires that one be prepared to pay the price in terms of an additional workload and the absence of recognition. But by saying this, Beckerian sociology turns sociology's usual questions upside down since change, not continuity, is foregrounded. Becker, "The Power of Inertia," in *Propos sur l'art*, 59ff.

9. Becker, *Propos sur l'art*, 31.

10. Ibid., 32.

11. Redfield, *Folk Culture of Yucatan*, 132. Quoted in Becker, *Outsiders*, 80.

12. In any case no subject is illegitimate for sociology. Nor are there any "small subjects," every situation bearing as much general information on the collective dynamics of interactions as any other.

13. Becker, *Outsiders*, 82.

14. "What kinds of public spaces were there for jazz in Chicago at that time? Who went there, and what were they looking for? What kinds of music did we find to play, given the circumstances? . . . At the time, there were very few places that were explicitly devoted to jazz and clearly advertised the fact with a sign marked 'Jazz Club,' where you went because a specific kind of jazz was played there, and that was what you wanted to hear. . . . I didn't play in any of those places that offered jazz, any more than most of my colleagues. We performed (we would have said: 'we worked') in various places intended for leisure activities and were supposed to be profitable, and that took different forms. We played for private parties organized by individuals or by groups for the pleasure of their members or their hosts: most of these were for marriages, bar mitzvahs, or galas given by associations for their members. They usually took place in venues rented for the occasion: leisure clubs, hotel dance halls, an ethnic community's meeting room, the social room at a church. The host generally provided the food, which was usually made by a caterer, and the music was played by a small band that was hired for the occasion (usually without their employers knowing about it) and that might very well have never played together before. . . . What we played on such occasions varied depending on the class, age, and ethnic origin of the group attending the party. The wedding rituals varied substantially depending on the ethnic community, which often required a specific kind of music. If we were playing for an Italian wedding, we had to be ready to play 'Come Back to Sorrento,' 'O sole mio,' and a few tarantellas that the old people loved. For a Polish marriage, there had to be polkas" (Becker, *Paroles et musique*, 15–17).

15. Becker, *Outsiders*, 83.

16. Ibid., 85–86.

17. Ibid., 99.

18. Ibid., 87.

19. This kind of perspective on social life owes a great deal to Herbert Blumer, who, according to Becker, developed symbolic interactionism or was at least the first to speak about it as a viewpoint, as a "theory," and as an alternative to his three "pet peeves": the theory of instincts, the "stimulus-response" theory, and the theory of culture. See H. S. Becker, "Quelques idées sur l'interaction," in Blanc and Pessin, *L'art du terrain*, 245ff.

20. Ibid., 248–49.

21. Ibid., 247.

CHAPTER 4

1. "The empirical world can be seen only through a schema or a representation that one has of it. The process of scientific research is oriented and informed *as a whole* by the underlying image of the empirical world that is used. This image determines the choice and the formulation of problems, defines what a given is, the means to be used to obtain it, the types of relationships that the givens maintain among themselves, and the mold in which propositions are cast" (Blumer, *Symbolic Interactionism*, 24).

2. Becker, *Tricks of the Trade*, 11.

3. Ibid., 48.

4. Ibid., 44.

5. Ibid., 45.

6. Ibid.

7. Ibid., 46.

8. Ibid., 31.

9. Becker, *Propos sur l'art*, 27–28.

10. Ibid., 28–29.

11. H. S. Becker, "Quelques idées sur l'interaction," in Blanc and Pessin, *L'art du terrain*, 254–55.

12. See Becker, *Tricks of the Trade*, 58–59.

13. Ibid., 60–61.

14. Vaughan, *Uncoupling*.

15. Becker, *Tricks of the Trade*, 61.

16. Ibid., 89.

17. "I position myself in the intellectual heritage of Robert E. Park, the founder of what has come to be called the Chicago School of sociology. Park was a convinced defender of what we now call ethnographic methods. But he also defended quantitative methods, in particular ecological ones. I am fully in agreement with him on this point, and in

my view, the resemblances between these two types of methods are at least as important as the differences, if not more. I think in fact that the same epistemological arguments support both of them and guarantee their scientific character" (H. S. Becker, "Epistémologie de la recherche qualitative," in Blanc and Pessin, *L'art du terrain*, 60).

18. Becker, *Tricks of the Trade*, 61.

19. Becker cites the example of studies devoted to revolutionary phenomena, whose researchers generally and spontaneously choose to collect knowledge about the American, French, Russian, Chinese, and sometimes English revolutions, sincerely thinking that this gives them sufficient material; however, such a focus neglects the hundreds of revolutions that have taken place in other times and other places, which constitute at least three quarters of humanity's revolutionary experience. Ibid., 84.

20. See ibid., 86.

21. Ibid.

22. Ibid., 144.

23. See ibid., 139.

24. Ibid., 195.

25. Ibid., 25.

26. On these points, Becker refers to the work of Charles Ragin and, before him, that of George Boole. See ibid., 185.

CHAPTER 5

1. Becker, Geer, and Hughes, *Making the Grade*.

2. Becker, *Tricks of the Trade*, 100.

3. Ibid., 83.

4. Cf. Becker, *Writing for Social Scientists*.

5. Becker, *Tricks of the Trade*, 85.

6. Ibid., 96.

7. Perec, *Les choses: Une histoire des années soixante*; Perec, *La vie: Mode d'emploi*; and Perec, *Tentative d'épuisement d'un lieu parisien*.

8. Becker, *Paroles et musique*, 69.

9. Agee and Evans, *Let Us Now Praise Famous Men*.

10. See Becker, *Tricks of the Trade*, 80ff.

11. Becker, *Paroles et musique*, 70.

12. A general presentation of his various contributions to thought on photography can be found in Henri Peretz, "Que faire de la photographie, ou: Howard Becker entre sociologie et photographie," in Blanc and Pessin, *L'art du terrain*, 171ff.

13. Becker, *Propos sur l'art*, 181.

14. Becker, *Paroles et musique*, 41.

15. Meyer, *Emotion and Meaning in Music*; and Smith, *Poetic Closure*.

16. Becker, *Paroles et musique*, 43.

17. Ibid., 46ff.

18. Becker, *Doing Things Together*, 301.

19. Becker, *Paroles et musique*, 89. This volume also includes a notable attempt to make sociological use of Italo Calvino's literary work.

CHAPTER 6

1. Molotch, "Going Out," 231.

2. Becker, *Tricks of the Trade*, 16.

3. Ibid. (quoting Molotch, "Going Out," 231).

4. Becker, *Paroles et musique*, 89.

5. H. S. Becker, "Making It Up as You Go Along: How I Wrote *Art Worlds*" (paper presented at the University of Grenoble, April 29, 2004).

6. See H. S. Becker, "The Work Itself" (paper presented at a conference on the sociology of art, Grenoble, November 1999).

7. In many studies by doctoral candidates and even by the most seasoned academics, we find the idea that the notions of "world" (Becker) and "field" (Bourdieu) are practically interchangeable. The only thing that differentiates them is said to be that the former emphasizes cooperation, while the latter emphasizes conflict. Thus, it is supposed to be merely a matter of nuance. This interpretation is absolutely wrong. These two notions are completely contradictory, not only because, as I have noted, the term "cooperation" signifies only "do together" and does not exclude any form of conflict, but also for a whole series of reasons of which I shall mention here only the principal ones. The notion of "field" is indebted to a generative principle of social life, that of the polemical fracture of societies, and to the essential reality, in diverse historical forms, of the confrontation between social classes, whereas for Becker, the possible existence of social classes does not authorize us to make their struggle such a generative principle. Also, the points of view are opposed regarding the value of the truth of the knowledge that the actors may have of their own situation and their own action. For Bourdieu, the truth of interaction is *illusio*, that is, error or ideology, whereas for Becker, it is "shared understandings," symbolic knowledge and acts of recognition that offer everyone the opportunity to base himself on other people's representations to construct his own action. "World" and

"field" are also contradictory concepts because the activity of sociology does not consist in extracting oneself from common knowledge but in immersing oneself in it and working on the basis of it. Another difference between the approaches is that the notions of disposition and career proceed from opposed logics. For these reasons and because of the diverse consequences they imply, these two approaches and, in particular, these two notions cannot be identified or even brought closer to one another and used interchangeably. For Becker, the notion of field is a "mystical notion," and concerning the domain of artistic activity, Bourdieu's problem is that he did not understand the pleasure of art.

APPENDIX A

1. This article first appeared in French: Howard S. Becker and Alain Pessin, "Dialogue sur les notions de Monde et de Champ," *Sociologie de l'art*, n.s., 8 (2006): 165–80. The English translation here, by Howard S. Becker, appeared as Howard S. Becker and Alain Pessin, "A Dialogue on the Ideas of 'World' and 'Field,'" *Sociological Forum* 21, no. 2 (2006): 275–86, and is reproduced with permission of Springer.

2. Bourdieu, *Esquisse pour une auto-analyse.*

3. Bourdieu, *Rules of Art*, 9–10.

4. See Gilmore, "Coordination and Convention."

5. Simmel, "'The Secret' and the Secret Society."

APPENDIX B

1. This piece first appeared in *Sociologie de l'art*, n.s., 8 (2006): 9–10.

APPENDIX C

1. Pessin, *La rêverie anarchiste*, 170ff.

2. Ibid., 170. All the following quotations are from this source.

Bibliography

Works by Howard S. Becker

Becker, Howard S. *Art Worlds*. Berkeley: University of California Press, 1982; 25th anniversary ed., updated and expanded, Berkeley: University of California Press, 2008. Translated as *Les mondes de l'art* (Paris: Flammarion, 1988).

———. *Doing Things Together*. Evanston, IL: Northwestern University Press, 1986.

———. *Outsiders: Studies in the Sociology of Deviance*. New York: Free Press, 1963. Translated as *Outsiders: Etudes de sociologie de la déviance* (Paris: A. M. Métaillé, 1985).

———. *Paroles et musique*. Paris: L'Harmattan, 2003. This book includes the CD *À Grenoble* with Howard Becker (piano) and Benoît Cancoin (bass).

———. *Propos sur l'art*. Paris: L'Harmattan, 1999.

———. *Sociological Work: Method and Substance*. Chicago: Aldine, 1970.

———. *Tricks of the Trade: How to Think about Your Research While You're Doing It*. Chicago: University of Chicago Press, 1998. Translated as *Les ficelles du métier: Comment conduire sa recherche en sciences sociales* (Paris: La Découverte, 2002).

———. *Writing for Social Scientists*. Chicago: University of Chicago Press, 1986.

Becker, Howard S., Blanche Geer, and Everett C. Hughes. *Making the Grade: The Academic Side of College Life.* New Brunswick, NJ: Transaction, 1994.

Becker, Howard S., Blanche Geer, Everett C. Hughes, and Anselm L. Strauss. *Boys in White: Student Culture in Medical School.* 1961. New Brunswick, NJ: Transaction, 1977.

Faulkner, Robert R., and Howard S. Becker. *"Do You Know . . . ?" The Jazz Repertoire in Action.* Chicago: University of Chicago Press, 2009.

Other Works Cited

Agee, James, and Walker Evans. *Let Us Now Praise Famous Men.* New York: Houghton Mifflin, 1941. Translated as *Louons maintenant les grands hommes: Alabama, trois familles de métayers en 1936* (Paris: Plon, 1972).

Blanc, Alain, and Alain Pessin. *L'art du terrain: Mélanges offerts à Howard S. Becker.* Paris: L'Harmattan, 2004.

Blumer, Herbert. *Symbolic Interactionism.* Englewood Cliffs, NJ: Prentice-Hall, 1969.

Bourdieu, Pierre. *Esquisse pour une auto-analyse.* Paris: Raisons d'agir éditions, 2004.

———. *The Rules of Art: Genesis and Structure of the Literary Field.* Stanford, CA: Stanford University Press, 1996.

Chapoulie, Jean-Michel. *La tradition sociologique de Chicago.* Paris: Seuil, 2001.

Gilmore, Samuel. "Coordination and Convention: The Organization of the Concert World." *Symbolic Interaction* 10 (1987): 209–28.

Gopnick, Adam. "The Outside Game." *New Yorker,* January 12, 2015, 26–31.

Hughes, Everett C. *Le regard sociologique.* Paris: Ecole des Hautes Etudes en Sciences Sociales, 1996.

Majastre, Jean-Olivier, and Alain Pessin, eds. *Vers une sociologie des œuvres.* 2 vols. Paris: L'Harmattan, 2001.

Meyer, Leonard B. *Emotion and Meaning in Music.* Chicago: University of Chicago Press, 1956.

Molotch, Harvey. "Going Out." *Sociological Forum* 9, no. 2 (1994): 221–39.

Moulin, Raymonde. *Le marché de la peinture en France.* Paris: Minuit, 1967.

Perec, Georges. *La vie: Mode d'emploi.* Paris: Hachette, 1978.

———. *Les choses: Une histoire des années soixante.* Paris: Hachette, 1965.

————. *Tentative d'épuisement d'un lieu parisien*. Paris: Bourgois, 1982.

————. *Un homme qui dort*. Paris: Gallimard, 1991.

Pessin, Alain. *La rêverie anarchiste, 1848–1914*. Paris: Méridiens-Klincksieck, 1982.

————. *L'imaginaire utopique aujourd'hui*. Paris: PUF, 1992.

————. *Un sociologue en liberté: Lecture de Howard S. Becker*. Quebec: Les Presses de l'Université Laval, 2004.

Redfield, Robert. *The Folk Culture of Yucatan*. Chicago: University of Chicago Press, 1941.

Simmel, Georg. "'The Secret' and the Secret Society." In *The Sociology of Georg Simmel*, ed. Kurt H. Wolff, 307–78. New York: Macmillan, 1950.

Smith, Barbara Herrnstein. *Poetic Closure: A Study of How Poems End*. Chicago: University of Chicago Press, 1968.

Thomas, William, and Florian Znaniecki. *Le paysan polonais en Europe et en Amérique (1918–1920)*. Paris: Nathan, 1998.

Vaughan, Diane. *Uncoupling: Turning Points in Intimate Relationships*. New York: Oxford University Press, 1986.

Interviews

Allemand, Sylvain. "Rencontre avec Howard Becker." *Sciences humaines* 89 (December 1998): 38–41.

Diani, Marco. "Howard Becker, un classique de la sociologie américaine." *Sociétés* 12 (January–February 1987): 38–40.